STAND OUT

Evidence-Based Learning for College and Career Readiness

5

THIRD EDITION

STACI JOHNSON

ROB JENKINS

 **NATIONAL GEOGRAPHIC LEARNING** |  **CENGAGE** Learning·

Australia • Brazil • Mexico • Singapore • United Kingdom • United States

Stand Out 5: Evidence-Based Learning for College and Career Readiness, Third Edition
Staci Johnson and Rob Jenkins

Publisher: Sherrise Roehr

Executive Editor: Sarah Kenney

Development Editor: Lewis Thompson

Director of Global Marketing: Ian Martin

Executive Marketing Manager: Ben Rivera

Product Marketing Manager: Dalia Bravo

Director of Content and Media Production: Michael Burggren

Production Manager: Daisy Sosa

Media Researcher: Leila Hishmeh

Senior Print Buyer: Mary Beth Hennebury

Cover and Interior Designer: Brenda Carmichael

Composition: Lumina

Cover Image: Seth Joel/Getty Images

Bottom Images: Jay B Sauceda/Getty Images; Tripod/Getty Images; Portra Images/Getty Images; Portra Images/Getty Images; Mark Edward Atkinson/Tracey Lee/Getty Images; Hero Images/Getty Images; Jade/Getty Images; James Porter/Getty Images; LWA/Larry Williams/Getty Images; Dimitri Otis/Getty Images

For product information and technology assistance, contact us at
Cengage Learning Customer & Sales Support, 1-800-354-9706

For permission to use material from this text or product, submit all requests online at **cengage.com/permissions**

Further permissions questions can be emailed to **permissionrequest@cengage.com**

Student Book
ISBN 13: 978-1-305-65564-5

National Geographic Learning/Cengage Learning
20 Channel Center Street
Boston, MA 02210
USA

Cengage Learning is a leading provider of customized learning solutions with office locations around the globe, including Singapore, the United Kingdom, Australia, Mexico, Brazil, and Japan. Locate your local office at: **international.cengage.com/region**

Cengage Learning products are represented in Canada by Nelson Education, Ltd.

Visit National Geographic Learning online at **NGL.Cengage.com**
Visit our corporate website at **www.cengage.com**

Printed in the United States of America
Print Number: 09 Print Year: 2023

ACKNOWLEDGMENTS

Ellen Albano
Mcfatter Technical College, Davie, FL

Esther Anaya-Garcia
Glendale Community College, Glendale, AZ

Carol Bellamy
Prince George's Community College, Largo, MD

Gail Bier
Atlantic Technical College, Coconut Creek, FL

Kathryn Black
Myrtle Beach Family Learning Center, Myrtle Beach, SC

Claudia Brantley
College of Southern Nevada, Las Vegas, NV

Dr. Joan-Yvette Campbell
Lindsey Hopkins Technical College, Miami, FL

Maria Carmen Iglesias
Miami Senior Adult Educational Center, Miami, FL

Lee Chen
Palomar College, San Marcos, CA

Casey Cahill
Atlantic Technical College, Coconut Creek, FL

Maria Dillehay
Burien Job Training and Education Center, Goodwill, Seattle, WA

Irene Fjaerestad
Olympic College, Bremerton, WA

Eleanor Forfang-Brockman
Tarrant County College, Fort Worth, Texas

Jesse Galdamez
San Bernardino Adult School, San Bernardino, CA

Anna Garoz
Lindsey Hopkins Technical Education Center, Miami, FL

Maria Gutierrez
Miami Sunset Adult, Miami, FL

Noel Hernandez
Palm Beach County Public Schools, Palm Beach County, FL

Kathleen Hiscock
Portland Adult Education, Portland, ME

Frantz Jean-Louis
The English Center, Miami, FL

Annette Johnson
Sheridan Technical College, Hollywood, FL

Ginger Karaway
Gateway Technical College, Kenosha, WI

Judy Martin-Hall
Indian River State College, Fort Pierce, FL

Toni Molinaro
Dixie Hollins Adult Education Center, St Petersburg, FL

Tracey Person
Cape Cod Community College, Hyannis, MA

Celina Paula
Miami-Dade County Public Schools, Miami, FL

Veronica Pavon-Baker
Miami Beach Adult, Miami, FL

Ileana Perez
Robert Morgan Technical College, Miami, FL

Neeta Rancourt
Atlantic Technical College, Coconut Creek, FL

Brenda Roland
Joliet Junior College, Joliet, IL

Hidelisa Sampson
Las Vegas Urban League, Las Vegas, NV

Lisa Schick
James Madison University, Harrisonburg, VA

Rob Sheppard
Quincy Asian Resources, Quincy, MA

Sydney Silver
Burien Job Training and Education Center, Goodwill, Seattle, WA

Teresa Tamarit
Miami Senior Adult Educational Center, Miami, FL

Cristina Urena
Atlantic Technical College, Fort Lauderdale, FL

Pamela Jo Wilson
Palm Beach County Public Schools, Palm Beach County, FL

ABOUT THE AUTHORS

Staci Johnson

Ever since I can remember, I've been fascinated with other cultures and languages. I love to travel and every place I go, the first thing I want to do is meet the people, learn their language, and understand their culture. Becoming an ESL teacher was a perfect way to turn what I love to do into my profession. There's nothing more incredible than the exchange of teaching and learning from one another that goes on in an ESL classroom. And there's nothing more rewarding than helping a student succeed.

Rob Jenkins

I love teaching. I love to see the expressions on my students' faces when the light goes on and their eyes show such sincere joy of learning. I knew the first time I stepped into an ESL classroom that this is where I needed to be and I have never questioned that resolution. I have worked in business, sales, and publishing, and I've found challenge in all, but nothing can compare to the satisfaction of reaching people in such a personal way.

Along with the inclusion of National Geographic content, the third edition of **Stand Out** boasts several innovations. In response to initiatives regarding the development of more complexity with reading and encouraging students to interact more with reading texts, we are proud to introduce new rich reading sections that allow students to discuss topics relevant to a global society. We have also introduced new National Geographic videos that complement the life-skill videos **Stand Out** introduced in the second edition and which are now integrated into the student books. We don't stop there; **Stand Out** has even more activities that require critical and creative thinking that serve to maximize learning and prepare students for the future. The third edition also has online workbooks. **Stand Out** was the first mainstream ESL textbook for adults to introduce a lesson plan format, hundreds of customizable worksheets, and project-based instruction. The third edition expands on these features in its mission to provide rich learning opportunities that can be exploited in different ways. We believe that with the innovative approach that made **Stand Out** a leader from its inception, the many new features, and the new look, programs, teachers, and students will find great success!

Stand Out Mission Statement:

Our goal is to give students challenging opportunities to be successful in their language-learning experience so they develop confidence and become independent lifelong learners.

TO THE TEACHER

ABOUT THE SERIES

The **Stand Out** series is designed to facilitate *active* learning within life-skill settings that lead students to career and academic pathways. Each student book and its supplemental components in the six-level series expose students to competency areas most useful and essential for newcomers with careful treatment of level-appropriate but challenging materials. Students grow academically by developing essential literacy and critical-thinking skills that will help them find personal success in a changing and dynamic world.

THE STAND OUT PHILOSOPHY

Integrated Skills

In each of the five lessons of every unit, skills are introduced as they might be in real language use. They are in context and not separated into different sections of the unit. We believe that for real communication to occur, the classroom should mirror real life as much as possible.

Objective Driven Activities

Every lesson in **Stand Out** is driven by a performance objective. These objectives have been carefully selected to ensure they are measurable, accessible to students at their particular level, and relevant to students and their lives. Good objectives lead to effective learning. Effective objectives also lead to appropriate self, student, and program assessment which is increasingly required by state and federal mandates.

Lesson Plan Sequencing

Stand Out follows an established sequence of activities that provides students with the tools they need to have in order to practice and apply the skills required in the objective. A pioneer in Adult Education for introducing the Madeline Hunter WIPPEA lesson plan model into textbooks, **Stand Out** continues to provide a clear and easy-to-follow system for presenting and developing English language skills. The WIPPEA model follows six steps:

- **W**arm up and Review
- **I**ntroduction
- **P**resentation
- **P**ractice
- **E**valuation
- **A**pplication

Learning And Acquisition

In **Stand Out**, the recycling of skills is emphasized. Students must learn and practice the same skills multiple times in various contexts to actually acquire them. Practicing a skill one time is rarely sufficient for acquisition and rarely addresses diverse student needs and learning styles.

Critical Thinking

Critical thinking has been defined in various ways and sometimes so broadly that any activity could be classified to meet the criteria. To be clear and to draw attention to the strong critical thinking activities in **Stand Out,** we define these activities as *tasks that require learners to think deeper than the superficial vocabulary and meaning.* Activities such as ranking, making predictions, analyzing, or solving problems demand that students think beyond the surface. Critical thinking is highlighted throughout so the instructor can be confident that effective learning is going on.

Learner-Centered, Cooperative, and Communicative Activities

Stand Out provides ample opportunities for students to develop interpersonal skills and to practice new vocabulary through graphic organizers and charts like Venn diagrams, graphs, classifying charts, and mind maps. The lesson planners provide learner-centered approaches in every lesson. Students are asked to rank items, make decisions, and negotiate amongst other things.

Dialogues are used to prepare students for these activities in the low levels and fewer dialogues are used at the higher levels where students have already acquired the vocabulary and rudimentary conversation skills.

Activities should provide opportunities for students to speak in near authentic settings so they have confidence to perform outside the classroom. This does not mean that dialogues and other mechanical activities are not used to prepare students for cooperative activities, but these mechanical activities do not foster conversation. They merely provide the first tools students need to go beyond mimicry.

Assessment

Instructors and students should have a clear understanding of what is being taught and what is expected. In **Stand Out**, objectives are clearly stated so that target skills can be effectively assessed throughout.

Formative assessments are essential. Pre- and post-assessments can be given for units or sections of the book through ExamView®—a program that makes developing tests easy and effective. These tests can be created to appear like standardized tests, which are important for funding and to help students prepare.

Finally, *learner logs* allow students to self-assess, document progress, and identify areas that might require additional attention.

SUPPLEMENTAL COMPONENTS

The **Stand Out** series is a comprehensive tool for all student needs. There is no need to look any further than the resources offered.

Stand Out Lesson Planners

The lesson planners go beyond merely describing activities in the student book by providing teacher support, ideas, and guidance for the entire class period.

- **Standards correlations** for **CCRS, CASAS,** and **SCANS** are identified for each lesson.

- **Pacing Guides** help with planning by giving instructors suggested durations for each activity and a selection of activities for different class lengths.

- **Teacher Tips** provide point-of-use pedagogical comments and best practices.

- **At-A-Glance Lesson Openers** provide the instructor with everything that will be taught in a particular lesson. Elements include the agenda, the goal, grammar, pronunciation, academic strategies, critical thinking elements, correlations to standards, and resources.

- **Suggested Activities** go beyond what is shown in the text providing teachers with ideas that will stimulate them to come up with their own.

- **Listening Scripts** are integrated into the unit pages for easy access.

Stand Out Workbook

The workbook in the third edition takes the popular **Stand Out Grammar Challenge** and expands it to include vocabulary building, life-skill development, and grammar practice associated directly with each lesson in the student book.

Stand Out Online Workbook

One of the most important innovations in the third edition of **Stand Out** is the online workbook. This workbook provides unique activities that are closely related to the student book and gives students opportunities to have access to audio and video.

The online workbook provides opportunities for students to practice and improve digital literacy skills essential for 21st century learners. These skills are essential for standardized computer and online testing. Scores in these tests will improve when students can concentrate on the content and not so much on the technology.

Activity Bank

The activity bank is an online feature that provides several hundred multilevel worksheets per level to enhance the already rich materials available through **Stand Out**.

DVD Program

The **Stand Out Lifeskills Video Program** continues to be available with eight episodes per level; however, now the worksheets are part of the student books with additional help in the lesson planners.

New to the third edition of **Stand Out** are two National Geographic videos per level. Each video is accompanied by four pages of instruction and activities with support in the lesson planners.

ExamView®

ExamView® is a program that provides customizable test banks and allows instructors to make lesson, unit, and program tests quickly.

STANDARDS AND CORRELATIONS

Stand Out is the pioneer in establishing a foundation of standards within each unit and through every objective. The standards movement in the United States is as dominant today as it was when **Stand Out** was first published. Schools and programs must be aware of ongoing local and federal initiatives and make attempts to meet ever-changing requirements.

In the first edition of **Stand Out**, we identified direct correlations to SCANS, EFF, and CASAS standards. *The Secretary's Commission on Achieving Necessary Skills,* or SCANS, and *Equipped for the Future,* or EFF, standards are still important and are identified in every lesson of **Stand Out**. These skills include the basic skills, interpersonal skills, and problem-solving skills necessary to be successful in the workplace, in school, and in the community. **Stand Out** was also developed with a thorough understanding of objectives established by the *Comprehensive Adult Student Assessment Systems* or CASAS. Many programs have experienced great success with their CASAS scores using **Stand Out**, and these objectives continue to be reflected in the third edition.

Today, a new emphasis on critical thinking and complexity has swept the nation. Students are expected to think for themselves more now than ever before. They must also interact with reading texts at a higher level. These new standards and expectations are highly visible in the third edition and include *College and Career Readiness Standards.*

Stand Out offers a complete set of correlations online for all standards to demonstrate how closely we align with state and federal guidelines.

IMPORTANT INNOVATIONS IN THE THIRD EDITION

New Look
Although the third edition of **Stand Out** boasts the same lesson plan format and task-based activities that made it one of the most popular books in adult education, it now has an updated look with the addition of National Geographic content, which will capture the attention of the instructor and every student.

Critical Thinking
With the advent of new federal and state initiatives, teachers need to be confident that students will use critical thinking skills when learning. This has always been a goal in **Stand Out**, but now those opportunities are highlighted in each lesson.

College And Career Readiness Skills
These skills are also identified by critical thinking strategies and academic-related activities, which are found throughout **Stand Out**. New to the third edition is a special reading section in each unit that challenges students and encourages them to develop reading strategies within a rich National Geographic environment.

Stand Out Workbook
The print workbook is now more extensive and complete with vocabulary, life skills, and grammar activities to round out any program. Many instructors might find these pages ideal for homework, but they of course can be used for additional practice within the classroom.

Media And Online Support
Media and online support includes audio, video, online workbooks, presentation tools, multi-level worksheets, ExamView®, and standards correlations.

CONTENTS

Numeracy/ Academic Skills	CCRS	SCANS	CASAS
• Pronunciation: Enunciate clearly • Develop research skills and ideas • Take notes • Focused listening • Prepare and deliver an oral presentation • Write a personal letter/e-mail	RI1, RI4, RI7, W2, W6, W7, W8, W9, SL1, SL2, SL3	**Many SCANS skills are incorporated in this unit with an emphasis on:** • Listening • Speaking • Social • Visualization • Cultural diversity	**1:** 0.1.1, 0.1.2, 0.1.4, 7.2.1 **2:** 0.2.1, 0.2.4 **3:** 0.2.3 **RE:** 7.44
• Reading • Interpret meanings of words in context • Develop categories • Write a paragraph • Focused listening • Take notes from lecture/oral sources • Interpret bar graphs • Research online	RI1, RI2, RI3, RI4, RI7, RI10, W2, W4, W7, W8, SL1, SL2, SL3, L1	**Many SCANS skills are incorporated in this unit with an emphasis on:** • Writing • Social • Negotiation • Leadership • Self-esteem • Self-management • Responsibility • Decision making	**VB:** 7.4.5 **1:** 7.4.2, 7.4.9 **2:** 4.1.9, 7.4.2 **3:** 7.4.2 **4:** 7.1.1, 7.1.2, 7.1.3, 7.4.2 **5:** 7.1.3 **RV:** 7.2.1 **RE:** 4.9.3, 7.2.1, 7.4.4, 7.4.5, 7.4.6 **TP:** 4.8.1, 4.8.5, 4.8.6
• Interpret meaning of idioms in context • Focused listening • Analyze and evaluate readings and budgets • Outline readings • Summarize reading passages and other sources of information • Make calculations • Create a budget	RI1, RI2, RI3, RI4, RI5, RI7, RI10, W2, W4, W5, W7, W8, SL1, SL2, SL3, SL6, L1, L2, L5	**Many SCANS skills are incorporated in this unit with an emphasis on:** • Mathematics • Social • Self-management • Responsibility • Problem-solving • Decision making	**VB:** 7.4.5 **1:** 1.5.1, 4.1.4, 2.5.5 **2:** 1.6.2 **3:** 7.4.2 **4:** 1.3.2, 7.4.2 **5:** 1.6.2, 7.4.2 **RV:** 7.2.1 **RE:** 4.9.3, 7.2.1, 7.4.4, 7.4.5, 7.4.6 **TP:** 4.8.1, 4.8.5, 4.8.6

CONTENTS

Numeracy/ Academic Skills	CCRS	SCANS	CASAS
• Organize sentences effectively to convey meaning • Focused listening • Read and interpret information • Scan for details • Outline prior to writing • Write two paragraph essay • Research through interview and on the computer • Make calculations • Interpret a chart	RI1, RI4, RI7, RI10, W2, W4, W5, W6, W7, W8, SL1, SL2, SL3, SL4, SL6, L3	**Many SCANS skills are incorporated in this unit with an emphasis on:** • Mathematics • Reading • Writing • Listening • Negotiation • Decision making	**VB:** 7.4.5 **1:** 1.9.5 **2:** 1.9.6 **3:** 1.9.8 **4:** 1.9.3 **5:** 1.9.2 **RV:** 7.2.1 **RE:** 4.9.3, 7.2.1, 7.4.4, 7.4.5, 7.4.6 **TP:** 4.8.1, 4.8.5, 4.8.6
• Understand and use parts of speech related to root words • Focused listening • Summarize reading passages • Scan for details • Skim for general ideas • Prepare and deliver an oral presentation • Research online	RI1, RI2, RI3, RI4, RI7, RI10, W2, W7, W8, SL1, SL2, SL3, SL4, SL6, L1, L3	**Many SCANS skills are incorporated in this unit with an emphasis on:** • Problem-solving • Self-management • Reading • Mathematics • Creative thinking • Responsibility • Visualization	**VB:** 7.4.5 **1:** 2.1.8 **2:** 1.4.3 **3:** 1.4.5 **4:** 1.4.6 **5:** 1.4.7, 1.4.8 **RV:** 7.2.1 **RE:** 4.9.3, 7.2.1, 7.4.4, 7.4.5, 7.4.6 **TP:** 4.8.1, 4.8.5, 4.8.6
• Analyze and use root words and related parts of speech • Focused listening • Make calculations • Interview others • Understand bar graphs • Read a spread sheet • Brainstorm • Use reference materials including a computer	RI1, RI2, RI3, RI4, RI7, RI10, W2, W3, W4, W5, W7, W8, SL1, SL2, SL4, SL5 SL6, L1, L2, L5	**Many SCANS skills are incorporated in this unit with an emphasis on:** • Mathematics • Reading • Self-esteem • Self-management • Responsibility • Problem-solving • Visualization • Decision making	**VB:** 7.4.5 **1:** 3.5.8, 3.5.9 **2:** 3.2.3, 3.2.4 **3:** 3.2.3, 3.4.5 **4:** 3.2.3 **5:** 3.4.3 **RV:** 7.2.1 **RE:** 4.9.3, 7.2.1, 7.4.4, 7.4.5, 7.4.6 **TP:** 4.8.1, 4.8.5, 4.8.6

CONTENTS

Numeracy/Academic Skills	CCRS	SCANS	CASAS
• Understand and use synonyms • Use reference materials • Research online • Use a computer to study • Take notes • Scan for main ideas and details • Brainstorm and construct arguments	RI1, RI2, RI3, RI4, RI7, RI8, W1, W2, W4, W5, W6, W7, W8, W9, SL1, SL2, SL4, SL5, SL6, L1	**Many SCANS skills are incorporated in this unit with an emphasis on:** • Social interaction • Negotiation • Self-management • Decision making • Writing	**VB:** 7.4.5 **1:** 1.2.4, 1.2.3, 1.2.5, 6.4.1, 6.4.3, 7.4.4 **2:** 1.3.1, 1.3.3 **3:** 1.6.3, 1.6.4, 1.7.1 **4:** 1.3.3 **5:** 1.6.3 **RV:** 7.2.1 **RE:** 4.9.3, 7.2.1, 7.4.4, 7.4.5, 7.4.6 **TP:** 4.8.1, 4.8.5, 4.8.6
• Interpret visual representations • Understand root words and suffixes • Analyze and evaluate • Understand and write directions and reports • Focused listening • Summarize reading passages	RI1, RI2, RI3, RI4, RI7, RI10, W2, W4, W5, W8, W9, SL1, SL2, L1	**Many SCANS skills are incorporated in this unit with an emphasis on:** • Social • Problem-solving • Visualization • Creative thinking • Negotiation • Teamwork • Leadership • Reading	**VB:** 4.5.1, 7.4.5 **1:** 4.4.8, 4.5.1, 4.5.4, 4.5.6 **2:** 4.5.7 **3:** 4.5.3, 4.7.2 **4:** 4.8.1, 4.8.5, 4.8.6 **5:** 4.6.4 **RV:** 7.2.1 **RE:** 4.9.3, 7.2.1, 7.4.4, 7.4.5, 7.4.6 **TP:** 4.8.1, 4.8.5, 4.8.6
• Interpret meanings of words in context • Focused listening • Scan for details • Skim for general ideas • Identify and paraphrase information • Analyze and evaluate • Interview others • Write a paragraph • Use transitional expressions in writing • Create visual representation to brainstorm • Write a speech	RI1, RI2, RI3, RI4, RI5, RI8, RI10, W1, W3, W4, W5, SL1, SL2, SL3, SL4, SL6, L5	**Many SCANS skills are incorporated in this unit with an emphasis on:** • Reading • Speaking • Responsibility • Cultural diversity • Decision making	**VB:** 7.4.5 **1:** 1.5.1, 5.3.6 **2:** 1.6.2, 5.2.2, 5.3.2, 5.7.1, **3:** 5.6.2 , 5.3.8, 7.4.2 **4:** 1.3.2, 5.3.7, 5.7.1, 7.4.2 **5:** 5.1.6, 5.7.1, 7.4.2 **R:** 7.2.1 **RE:** 4.9.3, 7.2.1, 7.4.4, 7.4.5, 7.4.6 **IP:** 4.8.1, 4.8.5, 4.8.6

For other national and state specific standards, please visit: **www.NGL.Cengage.com/SO3**

INTRODUCING
STAND OUT, Third Edition!

Stand Out is a six-level, standards-based ESL series for adult education with a proven track record of successful results. The new edition of *Stand Out* continues to provide students with the foundations and tools needed to achieve success in life, college, and career.

Stand Out now integrates real-world content from National Geographic

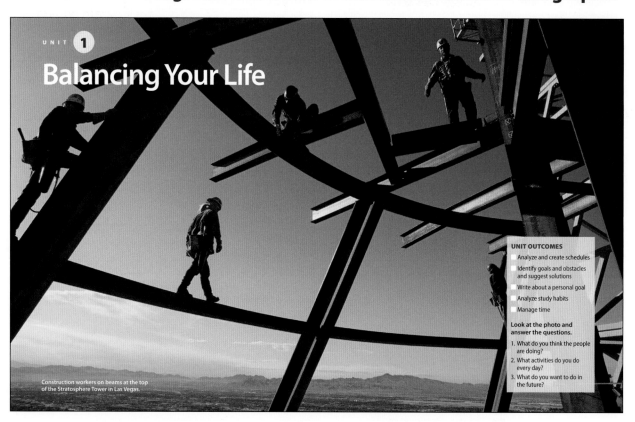

- *Stand Out* now integrates high-interest, real-world content from National Geographic which enhances its proven approach to lesson planning and instruction. A stunning National Geographic image at the beginning of each unit introduces the theme and engages learners in meaningful conversations right from the start.

Stand Out supports college and career readiness

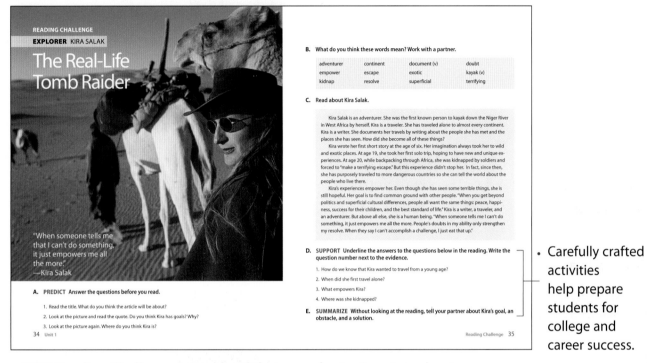

READING CHALLENGE

EXPLORER KIRA SALAK

The Real-Life Tomb Raider

"When someone tells me that I can't do something, it just empowers me all the more."
—Kira Salak

A. PREDICT Answer the questions before you read.

1. Read the title. What do you think the article will be about?
2. Look at the picture and read the quote. Do you think Kira has goals? Why?
3. Look at the picture again. Where do you think Kira is?

34   Unit 1

B. What do you think these words mean? Work with a partner.

adventurer	continent	document (v)	doubt
empower	escape	exotic	kayak (v)
kidnap	resolve	superficial	terrifying

C. Read about Kira Salak.

Kira Salak is an adventurer. She was the first known person to kayak down the Niger River in West Africa by herself. Kira is a traveler. She has traveled alone to almost every continent. Kira is a writer. She documents her travels by writing about the people she has met and the places she has seen. How did she become all of these things?

Kira wrote her first short story at the age of six. Her imagination always took her to wild and exotic places. At age 19, she took her first solo trip, hoping to have new and unique experiences. At age 20, while backpacking through Africa, she was kidnapped by soldiers and forced to "make a terrifying escape." But this experience didn't stop her. In fact, since then, she has purposely traveled to more dangerous countries so she can tell the world about the people who live there.

Kira's experiences empower her. Even though she has seen some terrible things, she is still hopeful. Her goal is to find common ground with other people. "When you get beyond politics and superficial cultural differences, people all want the same things: peace, happiness, success for their children, and the best standard of life." Kira is a writer, a traveler, and an adventurer. But above all else, she is a human being. "When someone tells me I can't do something, it just empowers me all the more. People's doubts in my ability only strengthen my resolve. When they say I can't accomplish a challenge, I just eat that up."

D. SUPPORT Underline the answers to the questions below in the reading. Write the question number next to the evidence.

1. How do we know that Kira wanted to travel from a young age?
2. When did she first travel alone?
3. What empowers Kira?
4. Where was she kidnapped?

E. SUMMARIZE Without looking at the reading, tell your partner about Kira's goal, an obstacle, and a solution.

Reading Challenge   35

- Carefully crafted activities help prepare students for college and career success.

- **NEW Reading Challenge** in every unit features a fascinating story about a **National Geographic explorer** to immerse learners in authentic content.

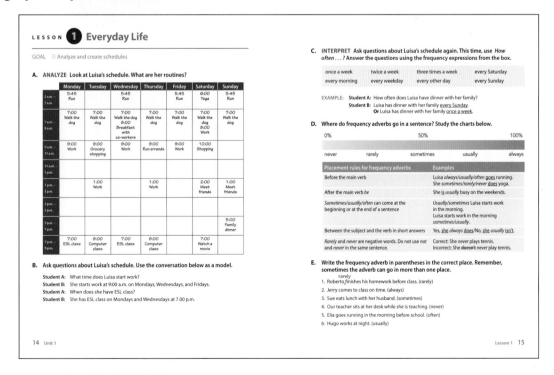

LESSON **1** Everyday Life

GOAL ■ Analyze and create schedules

A. ANALYZE Look at Luisa's schedule. What are her routines?

	Monday	Tuesday	Wednesday	Thursday	Friday	Saturday	Sunday
5 a.m. – 7 a.m.	5:45 Run		5:45 Run		5:45 Run	6:00 Yoga	5:45 Run
7 a.m. – 9 a.m.	7:00 Walk the dog	7:00 Walk the dog	7:00 Walk the dog 8:00 Breakfast with co-workers	7:00 Walk the dog	7:00 Walk the dog	7:00 Walk the dog 8:00 Work	7:00 Walk the dog
9 a.m. – 11 a.m.	9:00 Work	9:00 Grocery shopping	9:00 Work	9:00 Run errands	9:00 Work	10:00 Shopping	
11 a.m. – 1 p.m.							
1 p.m. – 3 p.m.		1:00 Work		1:00 Work		2:00 Meet friends	1:00 Meet friends
3 p.m. – 5 p.m.							
5 p.m. – 7 p.m.							5:00 Family dinner
7 p.m. – 9 p.m.	7:00 ESL class	8:00 Computer class	7:00 ESL class	8:00 Computer class	7:00 Watch a movie		

B. Ask questions about Luisa's schedule. Use the conversation below as a model.

Student A: What time does Luisa start work?
Student B: She starts work at 9:00 a.m. on Mondays, Wednesdays, and Fridays.
Student A: When does she have ESL class?
Student B: She has ESL class on Mondays and Wednesdays at 7.00 p.m.

14   Unit 1

C. INTERPRET Ask questions about Luisa's schedule again. This time, use *How often . . . ?* Answer the questions using the frequency expressions from the box.

once a week	twice a week	three times a week	every Saturday
every morning	every weekday	every other day	every Sunday

EXAMPLE: **Student A:** How often does Luisa have dinner with her family?
Student B: Luisa has dinner with her family *every Sunday*.
Or Luisa has dinner with her family *once a week*.

D. Where do frequency adverbs go in a sentence? Study the charts below.

0%		50%		100%
never	rarely	sometimes	usually	always

Placement rules for frequency adverbs	Examples
Before the main verb	Luisa *always/usually/often* goes running. She *sometimes/rarely/never* does yoga.
After the main verb *be*	She *is* usually busy on the weekends.
Sometimes/usually/often can come at the beginning or at the end of a sentence	*Usually/sometimes* Luisa starts work in the morning. Luisa starts work in the morning *sometimes/usually*.
Between the subject and the verb in short answers	Yes, *she* always *does*/No, *she* usually *isn't*.
Rarely and *never* are negative words. Do not use *not* and *never* in the same sentence.	Correct: She *never* plays tennis. Incorrect: She doesn't *never* play tennis.

E. Write the frequency adverb in parentheses in the correct place. Remember, sometimes the adverb can go in more than one place.

    rarely
1. Roberto finishes his homework before class. (rarely)
2. Jerry comes to class on time. (always)
3. Sue eats lunch with her husband. (sometimes)
4. Our teacher sits at her desk while she is teaching. (never)
5. Elia goes running in the morning before school. (often)
6. Hugo works at night. (usually)

Lesson 1   15

- **EXPANDED Critical Thinking Activities** challenge learners to evaluate, analyze, and synthesize information to prepare them for the workplace and academic life.

• **NEW Video Challenge** showcases **National Geographic footage and explorers**, providing learners with the opportunity to synthesize what they have learned in prior units through the use of authentic content.

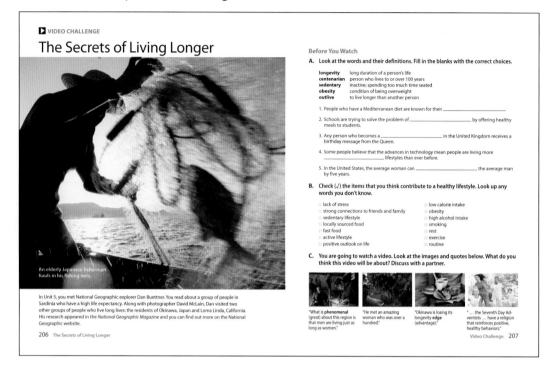

▶ VIDEO CHALLENGE

The Secrets of Living Longer

An elderly Japanese fisherman hauls in his fishing nets.

In Unit 5, you met National Geographic explorer Dan Buettner. You read about a group of people in Sardinia who have a high life expectancy. Along with photographer David McLain, Dan visited two other groups of people who live long lives: the residents of Okinawa, Japan and Loma Linda, California. His research appeared in the *National Geographic Magazine* and you can find out more on the National Geographic website.

206   The Secrets of Living Longer

Before You Watch

A. Look at the words and their definitions. Fill in the blanks with the correct choices.

longevity	long duration of a person's life
centenarian	person who lives to or over 100 years
sedentary	inactive; spending too much time seated
obesity	condition of being overweight
outlive	to live longer than another person

1. People who have a Mediterranean diet are known for their _____

2. Schools are trying to solve the problem of _____ by offering healthy meals to students.

3. Any person who becomes a _____ in the United Kingdom receives a birthday message from the Queen.

4. Some people believe that the advances in technology mean people are living more _____ lifestyles than ever before.

5. In the United States, the average woman can _____ the average man by five years.

B. Check (✓) the items that you think contribute to a healthy lifestyle. Look up any words you don't know.

	lack of stress		low calorie intake
	strong connections to friends and family		obesity
	sedentary lifestyle		high alcohol intake
	locally sourced food		smoking
	fast food		rest
	active lifestyle		exercise
	positive outlook on life		routine

C. You are going to watch a video. Look at the images and quotes below. What do you think this video will be about? Discuss with a partner.

"What is **phenomenal** (great) about this region is that men are living just as long as women."

"He met an amazing woman who was over a hundred."

"Okinawa is losing its longevity **edge** (advantage)."

"... the Seventh Day Adventists ... have a religion that reinforces positive, healthy behaviors."

Video Challenge   207

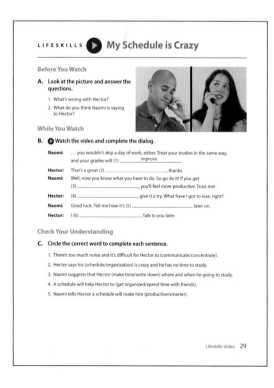

LIFESKILLS   ▶ **My Schedule is Crazy**

Before You Watch

A. Look at the picture and answer the questions.

1. What's wrong with Hector?
2. What do you think Naomi is saying to Hector?

While You Watch

B. ▶ Watch the video and complete the dialog.

Naomi: ... you wouldn't skip a day of work, either. Treat your studies in the same way, and your grades will (1) _____improve_____

Hector: That's a great (2) _____, thanks.

Naomi: Well, now you know what you have to do. So go do it! If you get (3) _____, you'll feel more productive. Trust me!

Hector: (4) _____ give it a try. What have I got to lose, right?

Naomi: Good luck. Tell me how it's (5) _____ later on.

Hector: I (6) _____. Talk to you later.

Check Your Understanding

C. Circle the correct word to complete each sentence.

1. There's too much noise and it's difficult for Hector to (communicate/concentrate).
2. Hector says his (schedule/organization) is crazy and he has no time to study.
3. Naomi suggests that Hector (make time/write down) where and when he going to study.
4. A schedule will help Hector to (get organized/spend time with friends).
5. Naomi tells Hector a schedule will make him (productive/smarter).

Lifeskills Video   29

• The **Lifeskills Video** is a dramatic video series integrated into each unit of the student book that helps students learn natural spoken English and apply it to their everyday activities.

Pages shown are from *Stand Out*, Third Edition Level 3

- **NEW Online Workbook** engages students and supports the classroom by providing a wide variety of auto-graded interactive activities, an audio program, video from National Geographic, and pronunciation activities.

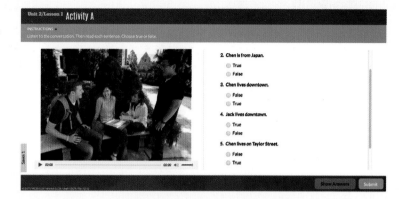

- **UPDATED Lesson Planner** includes correlations to **College and Career Readiness Standards (CCRS), CASAS, SCANS** and reference to **EL Civics** competencies to help instructors achieve the required standards.

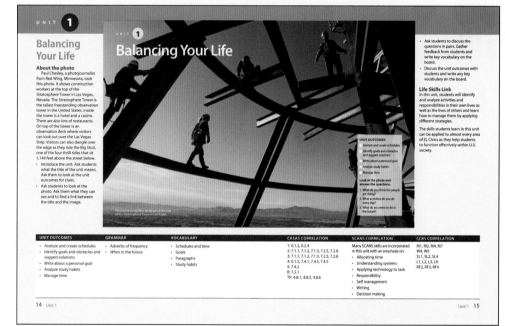

- **Teacher support** *Stand Out* continues to provide a wide variety of user-friendly tools and interactive activities that help teachers prepare students for success while keeping them engaged and motivated.

Stand Out supports teachers and learners

LEARNER COMPONENTS

- Student Book
- Online workbook powered by My **ELT**
- Print workbook

TEACHER COMPONENTS

- Lesson Planner
- Classroom DVD
- Assessment CD-ROM
- Teacher's companion site with Multi-Level Worksheets

Welcome

UNIT OUTCOMES

- Get to know people
- Talk about personal interests
- Write a personal message

LESSON ① Classroom community

🎧
CD
TR 1
A. **COMPARE** Read and listen to the conversation between Liam and Rani. Do you know people like them?

Hi, my name is Liam. I'm from France.

Nice to meet you, Rani. Why are you studying English?

I moved here so I could study at a university and learn how to be a graphic designer.

Nice to meet you, Liam. My name is Rani, and I'm from India.

I have been here for over twenty years. I stay home and help take care of my grandchildren while their parents work. I finally decided to improve my English so I can help them with their school work. What about you?

Agenda:
Dictation
Meet your classmates
Introduce your classmates

B. Introduce yourself to four classmates. Ask them where they are from and why they are studying English.

C. Who are the four classmates you met? Complete the table below.

Name	Country	Why are you studying English?

D. Read and listen to the conversation between Liam, Rani, and Haru. What does Liam say to introduce Haru to Rani?

E. Study the expressions below. Any response can be used for an introduction.

Introduction	Response
I'd like to introduce you to _____.	(It's) A pleasure to meet you.
I'd like you to meet _____.	(It's) A pleasure meeting you.
This is (friend's name) _____.	(I'm) Pleased to meet you.
Do you know _____?	(It's) Nice to meet you.
Have you met _____?	(It's) Good to meet you.

F. Work with a partner. Introduce him or her to four people in your class. Make sure you include the person's name, country, and why he or she is studying English in your introduction.

G. Read and listen to Haru as he introduces Kimla to the class.

Nice to meet you, Kimla.

I'd like you to meet Kimla. She came here with her family from Saudi Arabia four years ago. She has been studying English for three years now and would like to become a registered nurse. She hopes to apply to a nursing program at the end of this semester.

H. Choose two people who you have met in class today. Write introductions for them below. Use Haru's introduction in Exercise G as an example.

Name of classmate: _____

Information about classmate: _____

_____

_____

_____

Name of classmate: _____

Information about classmate: _____

_____

_____

_____

I. **APPLY** Choose one of the people from Exercise H to introduce to the class.

LESSON ② What are your hobbies?

A. INFER Look at the pictures of Haru, Rani, and Kimla. What do you think their personal interests are?

_____   _____   _____

_____   _____   _____

🎧 **B.** Listen to the conversation between Haru, Rani, and Kimla. Answer the questions below.

CD
TR 4

1. What kind of video games does Haru like to play?

   _____

2. What are three types of reading Kimla likes to do?

   _____

3. What type of photography does Rani like?

   _____

4. What doesn't Haru like to do?

   _____

5. How late does Kimla stay up reading?

   _____

6. What gift did Rani's son give her?

   _____

C. Share your answers with a partner.

D. People have many different types of interests. Look at the three categories of interests below. Can you think of some examples for each category?

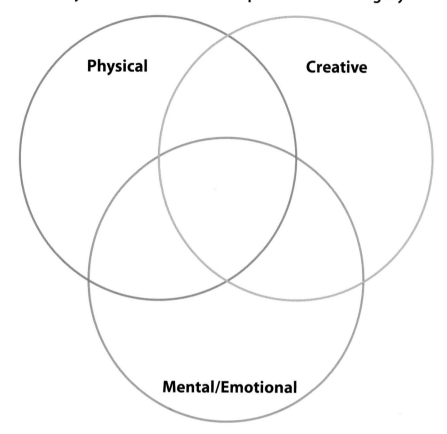

Physical   Creative

Mental/Emotional

E. **CATEGORIZE** Working with a small group, put each of the activities below into the circle you think is most appropriate. Some activities may belong in more than one circle.

cook	lift weights	run
do crossword puzzles	paint	swim
do yoga	play soccer	take pictures
draw	play video games	watch movies
knit	read	write

F. Think about your own personal interests. Write them in the appropriate categories below.

Physical: _____

Creative: _____

Mental/Emotional: _____

G. How would you ask people about their personal interests? Study the phrases below.

> What do you like to do in your free time?
> What are your hobbies?
> What are your interests outside of school/work?

H. COMPOSE Work with a partner. Write a conversation in which you discuss your personal interests.

Student A: _____

Student B: _____

Student A: _____

Student B: _____

Student A: _____

Student B: _____

Student A: _____

Student B: _____

Student A: _____

Student B: _____

Student A: _____

Student B: _____

Student A: _____

Student B: _____

I. In a small group, discuss your personal interests. When you have finished, share what you have learned about each other with the rest of the class.

LESSON ③ Dear friend

GOAL ▮ Write a personal message

A. Read the e-mail that Liam wrote to his family.

● ○ ○				
⇨ Send now	💾 Draft	🗑 Trash	📎 Attachment	✒ Signature

From: liam@ma1l.com
To: liamsdad@ma1l.com
Cc:
Subject: Living in the United States

Dear Mom and Dad,

Sorry it's been so long since my last e-mail. I've been so busy with work and school that I haven't had time to do anything else. I'm really enjoying being here in the United States. I've made a lot of great friends at my job and at school, and I'm really starting to feel like I belong here.

I think I told Dad when we spoke on the phone that I got a promotion at work. Instead of being a sales associate, I am now a sales manager. The added responsibility makes me a little nervous, but I think the bigger paycheck will make that go away! 😊

I just started a new English class, and my teacher, Mrs. Morgan, is great. She's pretty tough, but I think I'll learn a lot in her class. I'm hoping that by the end of this semester, my English will be good enough to start taking some graphic design classes. I've been practicing using my computer as much as I can in my free time, but I'm starting to need some professional guidance on how I can improve my design skills.

I hope you are both doing well! I really miss you and hope you can find some time to come out and visit. Mom, I really think you'd like it here.

Love,
Liam

B. This is a personal e-mail, not a formal e-mail. How can you tell that this e-mail is personal?

_____

C. INFER What do you think the following expressions mean?

1. feel like I belong _____

2. pretty tough _____

3. added responsibility _____

4. professional guidance _____

D. A personal message is a message that you write to a family member, a friend, or someone who you already know. Personal messages usually contain personal information and are written informally. Think of some people that you might write a personal message to. Who are they?

_____

E. There are many reasons for writing a personal message. Work in a small group to come up with a short list.

1. _____

2. _____

3. _____

4. _____

F. **DETERMINE** Read Liam's thank-you note. There are nine mistakes. Find the mistakes and correct them.

Dear Aunt Claire and Uncle Laurent
Thanks you so much for the crystal wine glasses you sent us for our aniversary. They is absolutely beutiful and I cant wait to has a dinner party so we can show them off. It was so thoughtful of you to think of us on our special day. I hope you are both doing well, and we hops to see you soon!
Kindest regards!
Liam

G. Rewrite Liam's note on a separate piece of paper. Correct the mistakes.

H. **Mrs. Morgan asked her class to choose someone they had just met in class and send them an e-mail. Read the e-mail that Rani wrote to Kimla.**

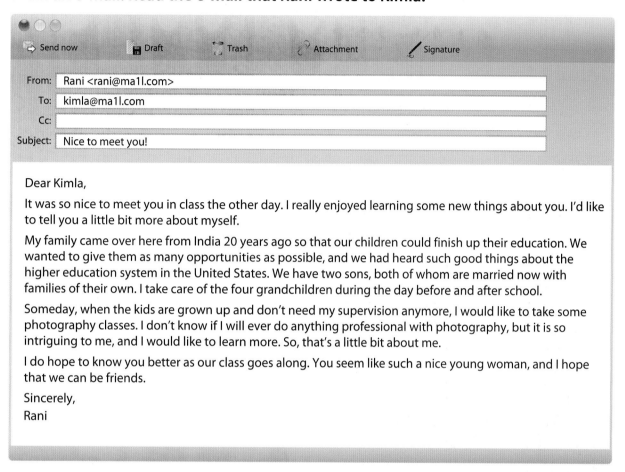

Send now	Draft	Trash	Attachment	Signature

From: Rani <rani@ma1l.com>
To: kimla@ma1l.com
Cc:
Subject: Nice to meet you!

Dear Kimla,

It was so nice to meet you in class the other day. I really enjoyed learning some new things about you. I'd like to tell you a little bit more about myself.

My family came over here from India 20 years ago so that our children could finish up their education. We wanted to give them as many opportunities as possible, and we had heard such good things about the higher education system in the United States. We have two sons, both of whom are married now with families of their own. I take care of the four grandchildren during the day before and after school.

Someday, when the kids are grown up and don't need my supervision anymore, I would like to take some photography classes. I don't know if I will ever do anything professional with photography, but it is so intriguing to me, and I would like to learn more. So, that's a little bit about me.

I do hope to know you better as our class goes along. You seem like such a nice young woman, and I hope that we can be friends.

Sincerely,
Rani

I. **COMPOSE** **Choose one of the classmates you recently met and write him or her a personal message about yourself on a separate piece of paper.**

Nowadays, keeping in touch is easier than ever.

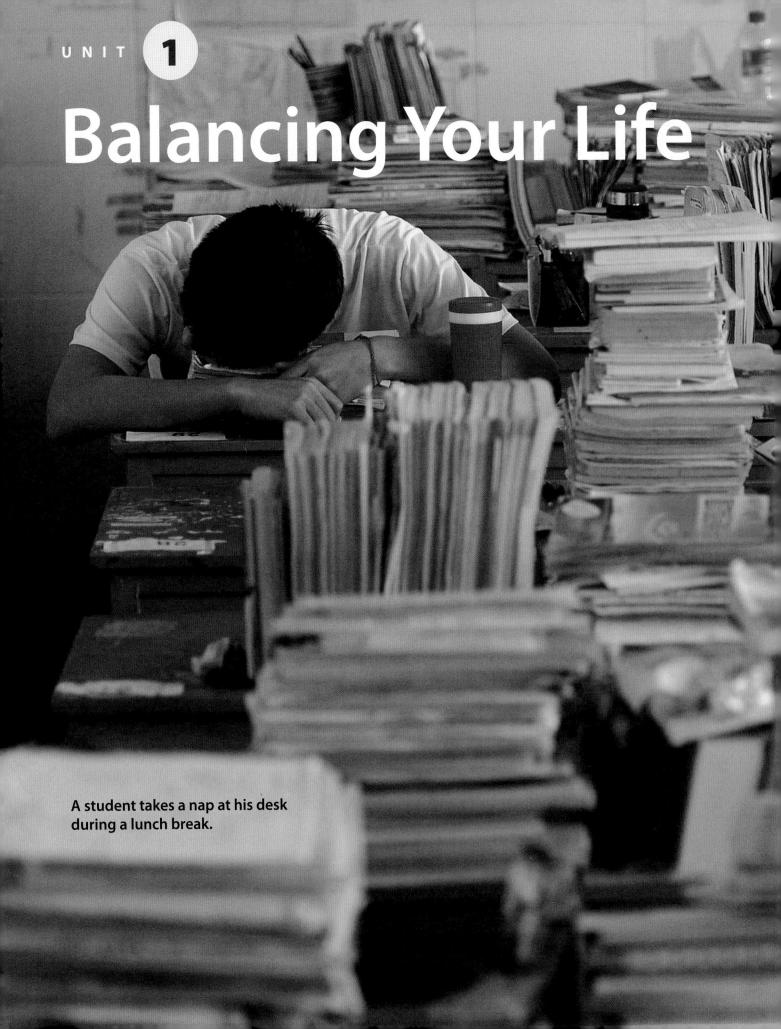

UNIT 1
Balancing Your Life

A student takes a nap at his desk during a lunch break.

UNIT OUTCOMES

☐ Identify learning styles

☐ Identify career paths

☐ Balance your life

☐ Identify and prioritize goals

☐ Motivate yourself

Look at the photo and answer the questions.

1. Why do you think this student is taking a nap?

2. What job do you think this student wants in the future?

Vocabulary Builder

A. Look at the pictures and read the information. What can you learn about the students?

Name: Carl
Learning style: visual
Career path: graphic designer
Motivation: financial

Name: Gloria
Learning style: visual
Career path: photographer
Motivation: joy

Name: Akira
Learning style: tactile/kinesthetic
Career path: computer programmer
Motivation: fun

Name: Abir
Learning style: auditory
Career path: registered nurse
Motivation: time with family

B. What do you think each expression means? Write your own thoughts.

1. learning style: _____

2. career path: _____

3. motivation: _____

C. **INFER** Below are groups of words that you will be working with in this unit. Make your best guess as to which topic in the box goes with each group. Topics can be used more than once.

career path	learning style	multiple intelligences
goal setting	motivation	

1. _____

    auditory

    tactile/kinesthetic

    visual

2. _____

    earning power

    pursue

    educational attainment

3. _____

    musical/rhythmic

    interpersonal

    intrapersonal

    logical/mathematical

4. _____

    naturalistic

    visual/spatial

    verbal/linguistic

    bodily/kinesthetic

5. _____

    achieve

    balance

    long-term

    motivate

    prioritize

    short-term

6. _____

    be flexible

    evaluate progress

    inspire

    monitor progress

    positive outlook

    support

D. Circle every word in Exercise C that you are familiar with.

E. Choose two new words from Exercise C that you would like to know the meanings of. Use a dictionary and write the word, part of speech, definition, example sentence, and any related words on a separate piece of paper.

LESSON **1** Learning styles

A. **EVALUATE** Check (✓) how you learn new skills. Do you . . .

☐ learn through seeing? ☐ learn through listening? ☐ learn through moving, doing, and touching?

B. Listen to a lecturer talk about three learning styles and take notes. Write down any key words you hear to describe each learning style.

Visual	Auditory	Tactile/Kinesthetic
seeing		
body language		
facial expressions		

C. Indicate the learning style next to each activity. Write *V* for *Visual*, *A* for *Auditory*, and *T/K* for *Tactile/Kinesthetic*.

1. touching objects _____

2. watching a video _____

3. looking at a diagram _____

4. reading a textbook _____

5. doing a science experiment _____

6. listening to a lecture _____

7. participating in a discussion _____

D. **EVALUATE** Check (✓) the learning style you think best describes you.

_____ visual _____ auditory _____ tactile/kinesthetic

E. What does *intelligence* mean? Write your ideas on a separate piece of paper. Then, look up the definition in a dictionary and write it below.

intelligence *n.* _____

F. **DETERMINE** Read about multiple intelligences. Underline the main idea in each paragraph.

According to psychologist Howard Gardner, there are eight different ways to show intellectual ability. These eight intelligences are described as visual/spatial, verbal/linguistic, logical/mathematical, bodily/kinesthetic, musical/rhythmic, interpersonal, intrapersonal, and naturalistic.

Visual/spatial learners tend to think in pictures. They like to look at maps, charts, pictures, and videos. They are good at such things as reading, writing, understanding charts and graphs, building, fixing, and designing.

Verbal/linguistic learners have the ability to use language. Unlike visual learners, they think in words. Verbal/linguistic learners are good at listening, speaking, writing, teaching, remembering information, and persuading others.

Logical/mathematical learners are good at using reason, logic, and numbers. These learners ask many questions and like experimenting. Logical/mathematical learners are good at problem solving, classifying information, figuring out relationships between abstract concepts, doing complex mathematical calculations, and working with geometric shapes.

Bodily/kinesthetic learners express themselves with their bodies through movement. By moving in the space around them, they can process and recall information. These learners are good at dancing, physical sports, acting, using body language, and expressing themselves with their bodies.

Musical/rhythmic learners have the ability to appreciate and produce music. These learners can immediately appreciate and evaluate the music they hear. Musical/rhythmic learners are good at singing, playing instruments, writing music, and remembering tunes they hear.

Learners with interpersonal intelligence are good at relating to others. They can see things from the point of view of others and they can sense people's feelings. They are good at communicating.

Intrapersonal intelligence, not to be confused with interpersonal intelligence, is the ability to be aware of one's own feelings. These learners are good at self-reflecting, and they try to understand their own hopes, dreams, strengths, and weaknesses.

Naturalistic intelligence has to do with understanding nature, that is, nurturing and relating information to one's surroundings. Naturalistic learners are sensitive to nature and have the ability to nurture and grow things.

G. INTERPRET Match each type of intelligence to a main idea.

1. visual/spatial _____   a. nurture

2. verbal/linguistic _____   b. be aware of one's feelings

3. logical/mathematical _____   c. use language

4. bodily/kinesthetic _____   d. think in pictures

5. musical/rhythmic _____   e. appreciate and produce music

6. interpersonal _____   f. express with movement

7. intrapersonal _____   g. relate well to others

8. naturalistic _____   h. use reason, logic, and numbers

H. EVALUATE Which types of intelligence do you think are strongest in you? Write down your top three in order. *1* is the strongest.

1. _____   2. _____   3. _____

I. How do you think the terms *learning styles* and *multiple intelligences* are related? Discuss your ideas in a small group.

J. Take a class poll on learning styles and multiple intelligences. Which learning styles and types of intelligence are most common among your classmates?

Musicians have the ability to appreciate and produce music.

LESSON 2 Career planning

A. What is the difference between a job and a career? Discuss the similarities and differences with a partner. Write your ideas in the table below.

Job	Career

B. Look up the words *job* and *career* in a dictionary. Write the definitions below.

job *n.* _____

career *n.* _____

C. **DETERMINE** Certain careers are associated with different intelligences. Look at the list of careers in the table and write which intelligence fits each category.

logical/mathematical	bodily/kinesthetic	musical/rhythmic
interpersonal	visual/spatial	intrapersonal
naturalistic	verbal/linguistic	

Intelligence	Careers
	architect, engineer, interior designer, mechanic
	journalist, lawyer, politician, teacher, translator, writer
	accountant, computer programmer, doctor, researcher, scientist
	actor, athlete, dancer, firefighter, physical education teacher
	composer, conductor, disc jockey, musician, singer
	businessperson, counselor, politician, salesperson, social worker
	philosopher, psychologist, researcher, scientist, writer
	conservationist, farmer, gardener, scientist

D. DETERMINE Look back at the three types of intelligence you think best describe your way of processing information on page 18. Using this information, choose two careers listed in Exercise C that you would be good at or interested in.

_____   _____

E. In a small group, discuss the two careers you chose in Exercise D and make notes. What steps do you think you would need to take to pursue one of these careers? Think about the education and training. Make notes of these steps.

F. In theory, the more education you have, the more money you can earn. Careers that require more education usually pay more. Look at the graph below. Which two things are compared?

_____ and _____

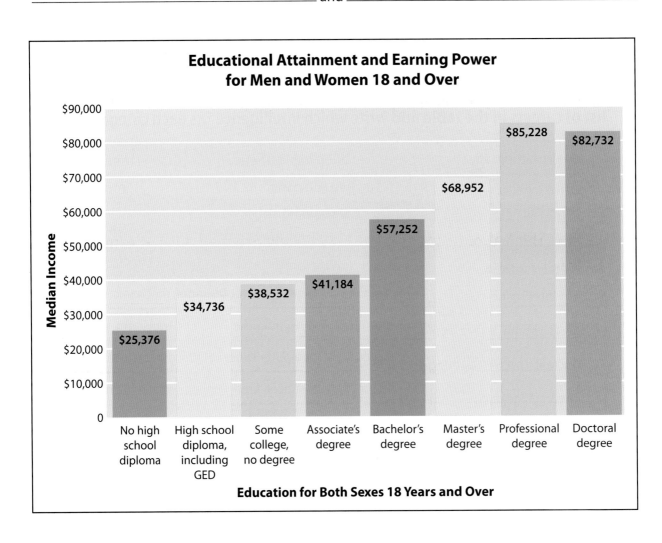

Educational Attainment and Earning Power for Men and Women 18 and Over

Median Income

- No high school diploma: $25,376
- High school diploma, including GED: $34,736
- Some college, no degree: $38,532
- Associate's degree: $41,184
- Bachelor's degree: $57,252
- Master's degree: $68,952
- Professional degree: $85,228
- Doctoral degree: $82,732

Education for Both Sexes 18 Years and Over

G. **With a partner, ask and answer the following questions. Use the information given in the graph in Exercise F to replace the underlined words and make new conversations.**

Student A: How much money can I make if I have <u>a master's degree</u>?

Student B: About <u>$69,000</u>.

Student A: If I want to make <u>over $70,000</u>, what level of education do I need?

Student B: You need <u>a doctoral or professional degree</u>.

H. **Listen to the conversation between a school counselor and Sonya. Take notes on the information you hear.**

1. Sonya's intelligences: _____

2. Career she is interested in: _____

3. Education she will need: _____

4. Time it will take to get her degree and credentials: _____

5. What are some other things you learned about Sonya from this conversation?

_____

_____

_____

I. **APPLY Think about a career path you might like to take. Fill in the information below.**

1. Your intelligences: _____

2. Career you are interested in: _____

3. Education and/or training you will need: _____

4. Time it will take you to follow your career path: _____

LESSON 3 Achieving balance

A. Sonya has many roles. Listen and take notes.

1. What are Sonya's roles?

   _____

   _____

   _____

Review: *Be*			
Subject	**Past**	**Present**	**Future**
I	was	am	will be
You, We, They	were	are	will be
He, She, It	was	is	will be

2. What was Sonya's role? _____

3. What will Sonya's role be? _____

B. IDENTIFY What are your roles? Write at least three statements.

I am a _____.

_____

_____

_____

C. What were your roles? Write at least two statements.

I was a _____.

_____

_____

D. What will your roles be? Write at least two statements.

I will be a _____.

_____

_____

E. COMPARE Share your responses with a partner. Are they similar or different?

F. Read what Sonya wrote and answer the questions below the paragraph with a partner.

Balance in My Life

When I was a little girl, I spent all my time playing with my two brothers. I just enjoyed doing whatever they were doing. Family was always very important to us. But as I grew older, I started working and studying more. It seemed like I was working all day, going to school every night, and studying whenever I had time. I didn't have any balance in my life. Now that I have my diploma, I don't study as much, but I still work a lot. I'm a manager at a restaurant, but I want to become an elementary school teacher. I am also a wife and a mother, and I want to spend more time with my family. I hope to find a job as a teacher where I can work fewer hours but still make enough money to help out. I will really enjoy being home with my family more and having more balance in my life.

1. How was Sonya's life different in the past from how it is now?

2. Is her life balanced right now? Why or why not?

3. What does she want to change in her life?

4. Do you think this change will make her happy? Why or why not?

G. Review the simple tenses.

Review: Simple Tenses				
Subject	**Past**	**Present**	**Future**	
He, She, It	studied	studies	will study	English every day.
We	put	put	will put	our studies first.
They	worked	work	will work	too many hours.

H. Complete each statement about yourself using the tense and verb in parentheses.

1. (*past*, spend) I _____.

2. (*present*, put) I _____.

3. (*future*, live) I _____.

I. Think about balance in your life. What are some things that are important to you? What are your interests? What activities do you do regularly? Make a list.

_____ _____ _____

_____ _____ _____

J. **EVALUATE** Think about how you balanced your life in the past, how you balance it now, and what you want for the future. Answer the questions below.

1. What was important to you in the past?

_____

2. What is important to you now?

_____

3. Do you spend enough time on the things that are important to you now? Why?

_____

4. What changes would you like to make for the future?

_____

_____

K. **COMPOSE** Using Sonya's paragraph in Exercise F as a writing model, write a paragraph on a piece of paper about balance in your life—past, present, and future.

L. Share your paragraph with a partner and ask for two suggestions about how to make your paragraph better. Write two suggestions for your partner's paragraph.

1. _____

_____

2. _____

_____

LESSON ④ Setting priorities

GOAL ▨ Identify and prioritize goals

A. Read the flier and answer the questions.

What is your BIG PICTURE?
Get what you want out of life!

Attend this goal-setting workshop to learn how to set long- and short-term goals and make your dreams a reality.

Peterson Hall, Room 15
Wednesday, October 7th from 5 to 9 p.m.

RSVP: bigpic@set0urg0als.com

1. What do you think *big picture* means?

_____

2. What is *goal setting*?

_____

3. Would you attend the workshop? Why?

_____

4. Write three goals you have set for yourself in the past.

   a. _____

   b. _____

   c. _____

5. Did you achieve your goals? Write *yes* or *no* next to each goal.

B. In a small group, discuss your answers to the questions in Exercise A.

C. Listen to the lecture on goal setting and take notes about the following on a separate piece of paper:

- Goal setting
- First thing you should do
- Seven types of goals
- Five tips for setting goals

D. CHOOSE Answer the following questions based on the notes you took. Circle the best answer.

1. Which of the following is NOT true about goal setting?

   a. It will improve your self-confidence.

   b. It helps motivate you.

   c. It makes you think about your past.

   d. It helps you choose a direction for your life.

2. What are the seven types of goals?

   a. financial, physical, attitude, pleasure, education, mental, family

   b. physical, career, family, financial, attitude, personal, education

   c. education, career, technical, financial, physical, attitude, pleasure

   d. financial, physical, career, family, education, attitude, pleasure

3. Why is it important to prioritize your goals in a list?

   a. It will be easy to know when you have achieved a goal.

   b. It will help you focus your attention on the most important goals.

   c. It gives them life.

   d. It will improve your self-confidence.

E. Sonya attended the goal-setting workshop and created a list of goals that she now keeps on her refrigerator.

I plan to be successful in my personal and professional life. I will be a highly educated elementary school teacher.

SHORT-TERM GOALS	LONG-TERM GOALS
• spend more time with my children	• get my bachelor's degree and teaching credentials
• exercise to reduce stress	• become an elementary school teacher
• enroll in community college	• get a master's degree
	• learn how to swim

F. Sonya's goals are prioritized (listed in order of importance). Do you think she put her goals in the right order? Discuss your ideas with a partner.

G. PRIORITIZE Think about where you would like to be ten years from now. Based on your thoughts, what are your long-term goals? Use the items below to help you clarify what your goals should be.

1. Write one goal for each category.

    Education: _____

    Career: _____

    Family: _____

    Financial: _____

    Physical: _____

    Attitude: _____

    Pleasure: _____

2. Number your three most important goals above in order of priority.

3. Based on these three long-term goals, what are some short-term goals you can set in order to help you reach the long-term ones?

    Short-term goals: _____

    _____

4. Prioritize your short-term goals. Write them in order. _____

    _____

LESSON ⑤ Motivation

A. What does *motivation* mean?

motivation (your own definition or one from a dictionary): _____

_____

B. GENERATE How can you motivate yourself to reach your goals? Work with a small group and make a list.

_____   _____

_____   _____

_____   _____

_____   _____

🎧 **C. Listen to Mrs. Morgan's students talk about motivating themselves. Take notes about what each person says.**

CD
TR 9

Carl: _____

_____

_____

Sonya: _____

_____

_____

Akira: _____

_____

_____

Gloria: _____

_____

_____

Abir: _____

_____

_____

Mario: _____

_____

_____

D. What idea for getting motivated does each person in Exercise C have? Share what you recall with a partner.

E. Below is a list of steps you can take to motivate yourself toward pursuing a goal. Check (✓) the steps you already do. Check (✓) the steps you would like to do.

I already do	I would like to do	Steps to motivate yourself toward pursuing a goal
		1. Write down your goals and put them in a place you will see them every day.
		2. Tell family and friends about your goals so they can support you.
		3. Tell yourself that you can do it.
		4. Keep a positive attitude.
		5. Be enthusiastic about your goals.
		6. When you slow down or don't have the energy to do anything, take small steps and continue moving forward. Don't stop.
		7. Evaluate your progress. Make a chart or do something to monitor progress.
		8. Don't be too fixed on one approach. Be flexible and make changes when needed.
		9. Read inspiring books.
		10. Take some time to refresh yourself.
		11. Exercise more to help your attitude. The better your health, the more positive your outlook.
		12. After you are motivated, motivate others.

F. COMPARE Share your list with a partner. Are there any steps that both of you would like to take? What are your differences?

G. Study the chart with your teacher.

		Past		
Subject	*will have*	**participle**		**Future event—Time expression**
I	will have	become	a teacher	**by** the time my kids are in school.
He	will have	been	a graphic designer (for five years)	**when** he turns 35.
They	will have	found	a job	**by** 2017.

We use the future perfect to talk about an activity that will be completed before another time or event in the future. present ✕ *future to be completed (perfect)* ✕ *future event with time expression*

Note: The order of events is not important. If the future event with the time expression comes first, use a comma.

Example: *By the time my kids are in school, I will have become a teacher.*

H. Mrs. Morgan's students wrote goal statements. Complete each statement with the correct form of the future perfect.

1. By the time I graduate from high school, I (do) _____ 500 hours of community service.

2. I (buy) _____ a new house when I retire.

3. When I turn 60, I (travel) _____ to over 20 countries.

4. We (put) _____ three kids through college by 2020.

5. I (become) _____ a successful business owner by the time I turn 40.

6. By the time I finish getting my degree, I (apply) _____ to three different graduate programs.

I. Write three goal statements for yourself on a separate piece of paper. Use the future perfect tense.

J. DECIDE Now that you have written down your goals, what are you going to do to keep yourself motivated? Write down three ideas on a separate piece of paper.

LIFESKILLS ▶ The presentation is due in two weeks

Before You Watch

A. Look at the picture and answer the questions.

1. What are Naomi, Hector, and Mateo doing?

2. What is Naomi showing Hector and Mateo?

While You Watch

B. ▶ Watch the video and complete the dialog.

Naomi: Come on, you guys. We have to do this (1) __presentation__ in two weeks. Two weeks! That's barely enough time.

Hector: OK, let's focus. The assignment was to do a presentation on jobs and (2) _____.

Mateo: The teacher gave a lecture about the relationship between education and (3) _____. Remember? So, maybe we could do something about that.

Naomi: Good idea! Let's do a presentation showing how an advanced degree can increase your (4) _____.

Hector: I like it. There have got to be some good (5) _____ on that.

Mateo: I think it would be good to show some of those statistics in the form of a graph or a (6) _____.

Check Your Understanding

C. Read the statements and write *True* or *False*.

1. Naomi, Hector, and Mateo have three weeks to do their report. __False__

2. Mateo takes notes while they talk. _____

3. Their report is about education and earning power. _____

4. Hector designs the bar graph. _____

5. Their chart shows that you earn more money if you have more education. _____

Review

Learner Log

I can identify learning styles.
■ Yes ■ No ■ Maybe

I can identify career paths.
■ Yes ■ No ■ Maybe

A. Indicate the learning style next to each activity. Write *V* for *Visual*, *A* for *Auditory*, and *T/K* for *Tactile/Kinesthetic* on the line.

1. analyzing a graph _____

2. listening to a discussion _____

3. listening to a lecture _____

4. participating in a dance _____

5. reading a journal article _____

6. touching objects _____

7. watching an online newscast _____

B. Complete each statement with a phrase from the box.

appreciates music	relates well to surroundings
expresses oneself with movement	thinks in pictures
is aware of one's own feelings	uses language
relates well to others	uses reason, logic, and numbers

1. A naturalistic person _____.

2. Someone with interpersonal intelligence _____.

3. A person who is kinesthetic _____.

4. A logical/mathematical person _____.

5. A person with visual intelligence _____.

6. Someone with intrapersonal intelligence _____.

7. A musical/rhythmic person _____.

8. A verbal/linguistic person _____.

C. Ask a classmate how they relate to the information below. Write his or her answers on the lines.

1. Types of intelligence: _____

2. Career interests: _____

3. What is important to you now? _____

4. What changes would you like to make for your future? _____

_____

Learner Log

I can balance my life.	I can identify and prioritize goals.	I can motivate myself.
■ Yes ■ No ■ Maybe	■ Yes ■ No ■ Maybe	■ Yes ■ No ■ Maybe

D. Write a paragraph about your partner on a separate piece of paper using the information from Exercise C.

E. Remember what you learned about goal setting. Without looking back in the unit, write four tips for setting goals.

1. _____

2. _____

3. _____

4. _____

F. Walk around the classroom and ask your classmates for suggestions on how to motivate yourself. Write five ideas below.

1. _____

2. _____

3. _____

4. _____

5. _____

G. Choose a verb from the box below and complete each goal statement with the correct form of the future perfect.

buy and sell	raise	program
apply	compete	

1. By the time I graduate from technical school, I _____ over twenty computers.

2. She _____ at least ten properties when she retires.

3. When he turns 65, he _____ two amazing children.

4. They _____ in their first triathlon by the year 2018.

5. By the time I get my master's degree, I _____ for forty jobs at companies all over the country.

Vocabulary Review

Use these words and phrases to help you complete all the exercises on this page. Some words may be used more than once.

achieve	evaluate	positive outlook
balance	inspire	prioritize
be flexible	long-term	pursue
earning power	monitor	short-term
educational attainment	motivate	support

A. Complete each sentence with the best verb. Note that some sentences can have more than one answer. Then, work with a partner and use the five questions for a discussion.

1. If you _____ your goals, you can focus on the most important ones first.

2. Have you ever created a chart to _____ your progress?

3. What career do you think you might _____?

4. How do you _____ yourself?

5. What goals have you wanted to _____ in the past?

6. Have you found family and friends to _____ you?

B. Write sentences about goal setting with the following terms.

1. balance: _____

2. be flexible: _____

3. positive outlook: _____

4. achieve: _____

C. Complete each sentence below.

1. To improve your earning power, you should _____

   _____.

2. If you want to achieve your goals, you must _____

   _____.

3. In order to best reach your long-term goals, you have to _____

   _____.

A. One of the fastest ways to research something is to search the Internet. For example, you might want to know how much money you can make at a certain career. What are some key words you could use to search for this information?

B. Conduct an online search to find out the following information for the career path that you chose in Lesson 2, Exercise I.

Career title: _____

Training needed: _____

Education needed: _____

Possible earnings: _____

C. The Bureau of Labor Statistics (bls.gov) publishes the *Occupational Outlook Handbook* every two years. This handbook gives information about hundreds of different types of jobs. In this handbook, you will find the following types of information: the training and education needed, earnings, expected job prospects, what workers do on the job, and working conditions.

The following topics are from the *Occupational Outlook Handbook*. Underline the topic you think would have information about your career.

Management, Business, and Financial Occupations	Service Occupations: Cleaning, Food, and Personal
Engineers, Life and Physical Scientists, and Related Occupations	Protective Service Occupations
Arts, Design, Entertainment, Sports, and Media Occupations	Sales Occupations
Education and Community and Social Service Occupations	Office and Administrative Support Occupations
Computer and Mathematical Occupations	Farming, Fishing, Forestry, and Transportation Occupations
Legal and Social Science Occupations	Construction Trades and Related Occupations
Health Diagnosing and Treating Practitioners	Installation, Maintenance, and Repair Occupations
Health Technologists, Technicians, and Healthcare Support Occupations	Production Occupations

D. Find the *Occupational Outlook Handbook* online at bls.gov/ooh. Search for the information about your chosen career.

Protecting the Places We Play

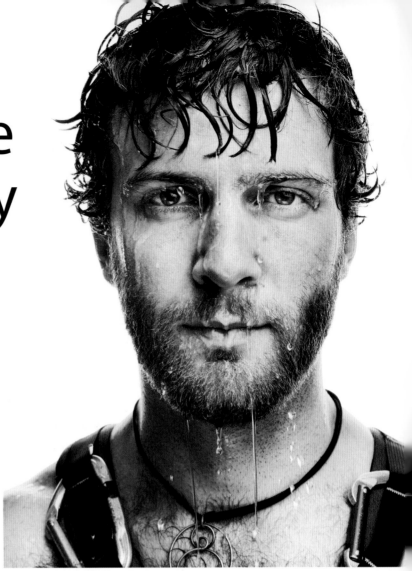

"The real challenge we're faced with today is not just exploring or doing exciting new things. It's also honoring the world we live in and protecting wild lands, wild animals, and the places we play."
— Trip Jennings

A. **PREDICT** Trip Jennings is a filmmaker and a professional kayaker. What do you think these two things could have to do with one another?

_____

_____

B. **INFER** Read the quote. What do you think he means by "honoring the world we live in"?

_____

_____

_____

_____

C. Read about Trip Jennings.

Trip Jennings is a filmmaker who loves to kayak. Or should that be a professional kayaker who loves to make films? Watching kayaking videos as a child, he decided that he wanted to be the one behind the camera. For years, he kayaked and produced whitewater (fast-moving and shallow stretches of water) kayaking videos, documenting some of the most beautiful places in the world. But to get to those amazing places, he had to travel through places where the environment had been destroyed. This caused him to rethink the purpose of his filmmaking.

In addition to being an award-winning filmmaker, kayaker, and adventurer, Trip is a conservationist. He spends his time working to protect rivers around the world. He also documents fossil fuel extraction, mining, and energy export in North America. To help get his word out, he runs a video production company called Balance Media. The company focuses on telling stories through videography for environmental and social justice organizations. He is also on the advisory board of Adventurers and Scientists for Conservation (ASC), which brings adventurers and scientists together to share data collected from around the world.

With everything that Trip has going on, it is often hard to stay balanced. When asked what a normal day is like for him, this is what he said: "I spend a fair amount of my time wishing for normal days, trying to find balance. I'm out and about for around half the year, traveling, filming, and working on conservation projects. In 2011, that led me to the Democratic Republic of the Congo, Canada three times, Mexico, and a number of trips within the U.S. The rest of the year I spend editing, fund-raising, and planning—all of the office work that makes the fieldwork possible and useful. So, half the year I'm waking up at sunrise in the wilderness, getting dirty, carrying cameras into the backcountry, and documenting beauty and destruction. The other half, I'm waking up and walking to my Portland office to click and drag most of the day."

D. Answer the questions on a separate piece of paper.

1. How does Trip work to "protect the wild lands, wild animals, and the places we play"?

2. Why do you think Trip decided to start making films about kayaking?

3. What caused his filmmaking purpose to change?

4. Think about Trip's "normal day." How is it is different from yours? Is it similar to yours in any way? How do you think he finds balance?

Personal Finance

A man plays the guitar in front of a coffee shop in a town center.

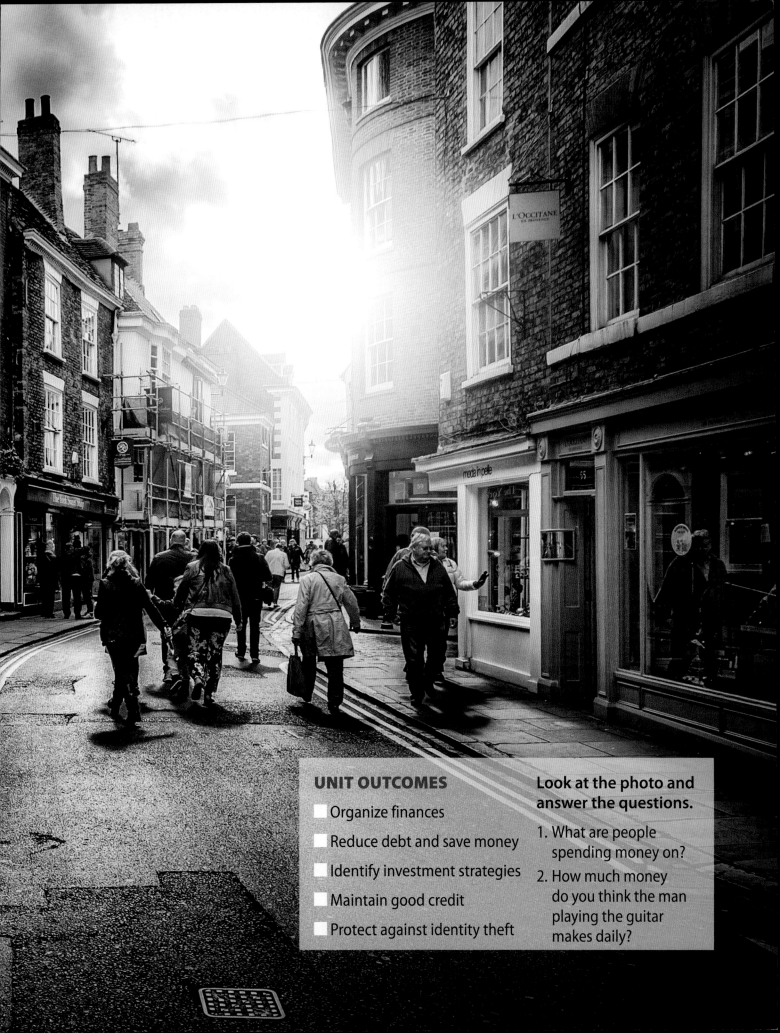

UNIT OUTCOMES

- Organize finances
- Reduce debt and save money
- Identify investment strategies
- Maintain good credit
- Protect against identity theft

Look at the photo and answer the questions.

1. What are people spending money on?

2. How much money do you think the man playing the guitar makes daily?

Vocabulary Builder

A. Kimla made a list of her financial goals. Read what she wrote.

> 1. I need to stop *impulse buying* and pay off my credit cards.
> 2. I want to stop *living paycheck to paycheck* and save enough money for a down payment on a house.
> 3. I want to increase my *purchasing power* by putting $200 a month into an emergency savings account.
> 4. I want us to start *living within our means*, so I can start giving $100 a month to charity.

B. INFER What does each italicized expression mean? Discuss them with your classmates.

C. Some phrases have special meanings. Often, if you try to understand the meaning of the individual words, you can understand the phrase. Talk to your classmates to discover the meanings of the following expressions.

1. budget cut	2. buy in bulk	3. capital gains
4. commit fraud	5. counterfeit checks	6. current income
7. delinquent accounts	8. false pretenses	9. unauthorized transactions

It's easier than ever to monitor your bank account, but be careful when making online transactions.

Secure payment

pay now

Credit Card allowed

D. INFER Look at the following sentences. Try to figure out the meanings of the underlined words by reading them in context.

1. The company declared <u>bankruptcy</u> when it ran out of money.

   Bankruptcy means _____.

2. I took out a loan at the bank and used my house as <u>collateral</u>.

   Collateral means _____.

3. The thought of starting a business was <u>daunting</u>, but he decided to do it anyway.

   Daunting means _____.

4. <u>Inflation</u> was so great that bread cost twice as much in June as it did in May.

   Inflation means _____.

5. His <u>investment</u> in the stock market has made him a millionaire.

   Investment means _____.

6. The company has no <u>liquid</u> assets; therefore, it can't pay its bills.

   Liquid means _____.

7. She paid the <u>penalty</u> of a large fine for lying on her income tax returns.

   Penalty means _____.

8. He <u>periodically</u> reviews his budget and makes changes when necessary.

   Periodically means _____.

9. Putting money in the stock market might be <u>risky</u> because you could lose it.

   Risky means _____.

E. Look back at Kimla's financial goals in Exercise A. Using some of the new vocabulary phrases, write four of your own financial goals.

1. _____

2. _____

3. _____

4. _____

LESSON ① Getting organized

GOAL ▨ Organize finances

A. Look back at the goals you wrote in Exercise E on page 41. Rewrite the goals below, giving each one a time frame.

EXAMPLE: _By the end of next year, I will have paid off my credit cards._

1. _____

2. _____

3. _____

4. _____

B. EVALUATE Do you know how much money you spend? Many people are not certain of the exact amount it costs them to live. Often, people don't include the expenses that come up occasionally in their personal budgets. Think about how you spend your money. Answer the following questions on a separate piece of paper.

1. Did you go on a vacation last year? How much did it cost?

2. Do you know how much you spend during the holidays every year? How much?

3. How often do you get your hair cut? How much does it cost?

4. How often do you pay car insurance premiums? How much is each premium?

C. Listen to a financial planner talking about how to organize personal finances. Write down the most important points.

CD
TR 10

1. _____

2. _____

3. _____

4. _____

5. _____

D. Compare your notes in Exercise C with a partner. Add any important points you missed.

E. ANALYZE After meeting with a financial planner, Kimla and her husband looked at all of their bank statements, credit card statements, ATM records, and receipts. Look at the worksheet below that they created. What do they still need to calculate?

MONEY OUT		
	Annual	Monthly
Mortgage/Rent		$2,200
Home maintenance fees		$250
Renters' insurance	$1,200	
Gas/Electric		$225
Water		$55
Telephone/Cell phone		$130
Food/Restaurants		$300
Medical/Dental		$145
Auto expenses		$240
Tolls/Fares/Parking		$60
Clothes/Shoes	$1,200	
Dry cleaning		$30
Hair/Manicure/Facial		$75
Kids' school	$1,800	
Training/Education	$300	
Income taxes	$2,100	
Internet		$50
Credit cards/Loans		$850
Subscriptions	$48	
Entertainment		$125
Cable/Satellite		$150
Vacations	$2,100	
Hobbies	$180	
Gifts	$800	
TOTAL		

Calculations

To calculate annual expenses, multiply monthly expenses by 12:

250	15	55	1300
$\times 12$	$\times 12$	$\times 12$	$\times 12$
3000	180		

To calculate monthly expenses, divide annual expenses by 12:

$3000 \div 12 = 250$ $180 \div 12 = 15$

$\underline{\hspace{1cm}} \div 12 = 55$ $\underline{\hspace{1cm}} \div 12 = 1300$

F. Calculate Kimla and her husband's annual and monthly totals.

G. Together, Kimla and her husband make $70,000 annually before deductions. Answer the questions.

1. How much do they have left over annually?

2. How much do they have left over each month?

3. Do you think Kimla and her husband live within their means? Why?

H. In the worksheet in Exercise E, some expenses are *fixed* (stay the same every month) and others are *variable* (change from month to month). With a partner, make a list of Kimla and her husband's fixed and variable expenses.

Fixed	Variable

I. **JUSTIFY** Look back at Kimla's financial goals on page 40. How much money does she want to start saving each month for emergencies and giving to charity? Does she have enough money in her budget for these items? If not, which expenses do you think Kimla and her husband can cut back on?

J. Create a worksheet like the one in Exercise E, listing all the monthly and annual expenses you have. Next to each expense, write *f* for a fixed expense or *v* for a variable expense. Look at the worksheet below to get you started.

	Annual	Monthly
Mortgage/Rent (f)		
Home maintenance fees (v)		
Gas/Electric (v)		
Water (v)		

LESSON ❷ Managing money

GOAL ▨ Reduce debt and save money

A. Read the ad.

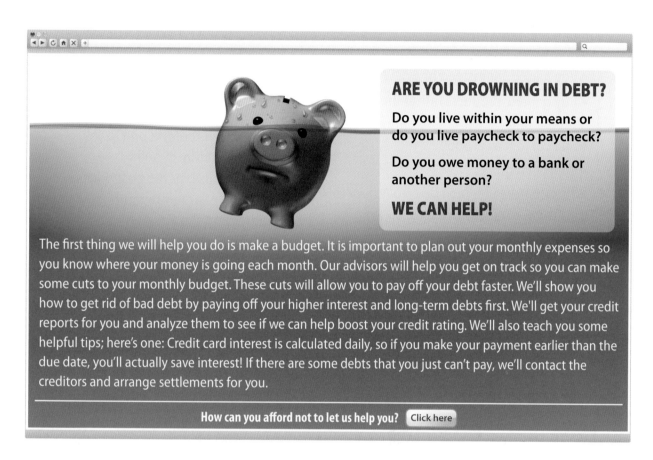

ARE YOU DROWNING IN DEBT?

Do you live within your means or do you live paycheck to paycheck?

Do you owe money to a bank or another person?

WE CAN HELP!

The first thing we will help you do is make a budget. It is important to plan out your monthly expenses so you know where your money is going each month. Our advisors will help you get on track so you can make some cuts to your monthly budget. These cuts will allow you to pay off your debt faster. We'll show you how to get rid of bad debt by paying off your higher interest and long-term debts first. We'll get your credit reports for you and analyze them to see if we can help boost your credit rating. We'll also teach you some helpful tips; here's one: Credit card interest is calculated daily, so if you make your payment earlier than the due date, you'll actually save interest! If there are some debts that you just can't pay, we'll contact the creditors and arrange settlements for you.

How can you afford not to let us help you? Click here

B. Answer the questions about the ad with a partner.

1. Who do you think wrote this ad? _____

2. What is the purpose of this ad? _____

3. Would you click on the bottom of the ad? Why? _____

_____

4. The ad mentions different ways to help people reduce debt. List four suggestions.

   a. _____

   b. _____

   c. _____

   d. _____

C. Read the tips on how to save money.

TIPS FOR SAVING MONEY

- Avoid impulse buying.
- Shop for bargains, not designer labels.
- Buy a used car instead of a new one.
- Buy generic products rather than brand names.
- Start or join a carpool.
- Collect coupons.
- Think before you buy: *Do I really need this?*
- Buy groceries at the market, not the convenience store.

- Increase your insurance deductible.
- Make meals at home instead of eating out.
- Make your own coffee in the morning.
- Pay your credit card in full each month to avoid paying interest.
- Plan ahead for food purchases so you can buy in bulk.
- Shop around for the best prices.
- Turn the heat temperature down in the winter and the air-conditioning temperature up in the summer.

D. Listen to Kimla and her husband, Derek, talk about saving money. Write *T* (*true*) or *F* (*false*) on the line before each statement.

CD TR 11

_____ 1. Kimla buys designer clothes.

_____ 2. Derek had been buying his coffee at a coffee shop.

_____ 3. Kimla had been paying high interest on credit cards.

_____ 4. Derek had been looking at new cars.

_____ 5. Kimla turns off the air conditioner before she goes to bed.

_____ 6. Derek called the insurance company to increase their deductible.

_____ 7. Kimla has never bought generic products.

_____ 8. Derek collects coupons.

E. ANALYZE Do you already follow some of the tips in Exercise C? Circle the ones you are familiar with. Underline the ones you would like to follow in the future.

F. **Study the chart with your teacher.**

Past Perfect Continuous Tense					
First event in past					**Second event in past**
Subject	*had*	*been*	**Verb + -ing**		
Kimla	had	been	buying	designer clothes	before she started bargain shopping.
He	had	been	buying	coffee at a coffee shop	before he began making it at home.
They	had	been	paying	a lower deductible	before they called the insurance company.

- We use the past perfect continuous to talk about an activity that was happening for a while before another event happened in the past. For the most recent event, we use the simple past tense.

- Remember to use a comma if you put the second event as the first part of the sentence. Example: Before she started bargain shopping, Kimla had been buying designer clothes.

G. **Think about your past behavior and how you have changed it to reduce debt and save money. Write four statements.**

EXAMPLE: *I had been eating out for lunch every day before I started making my lunch at home.*

1. _____

2. _____

3. _____

4. _____

H. **DECIDE Come up with three ways in which you are going to change your behavior to reduce debt and save money.**

EXAMPLE: *Tomorrow, I will start making my lunch at home.*

1. _____

2. _____

3. _____

LESSON ③ Investing wisely

A. In a small group, look at the following list of words and phrases. Which do you know? Find the meanings of those you don't know.

capital gains	convert	inflation	liquid	net appreciation
penalty	risky	value	vehicle	purchasing power

B. **COMPARE** Look at your meaning for *vehicle*. Compare your definition with the definition below.

vehicle: a way in which something is accomplished

C. **PREDICT** Based on the words and phrases you defined in Exercise A, what do you think the article below is about? Discuss your ideas with your classmates.

D. Read the article about investing money.

Due to inflation, money is worth less and less each year, so by not investing your money, you are actually losing money. In order to prevent inflation from destroying the value of your money, you need to invest. Let's take a look at some basic kinds of investments.

An investment can make you money in three basic ways. First, an investment can earn *current income*. Current income is money that you receive periodically, for example, every month or every six months. An example of an investment that provides current income is a certificate of deposit (CD) because interest is paid to your account periodically. A second way that an investment can make money is through *capital growth*. This is when the amount of money you have invested grows in value over time. When you sell the investment, you get your money back plus any increase in value. Examples of capital growth investments are stocks and other assets that you own, such as your home. Finally, a third way that an investment can earn income is through a combination of current income and capital growth. Examples include rental property and stocks that pay dividends, that is, extra or bonus amounts of money.

There are many different ways to invest your money, but let's look at five of the most widely used investment vehicles.

Probably the most popular investment vehicle is the savings account, which offers low minimum deposits, liquidity (the ability to withdraw and deposit whenever you want), and insurance protection. Because of these features, savings accounts pay relatively low interest rates. Another investment vehicle that is somewhat similar to a savings account in that it offers low interest rates and insurance protection is a certificate of deposit (CD). A CD requires that you put money in and leave it for a certain amount of time—three months, six months, a year, etc. Usually, the longer the amount of time you keep it in, the higher the interest. CDs are not perfectly liquid because early withdrawal of funds from a CD often results in a penalty. Another type of investment is a mutual fund where a number of investors put their money together to buy specific investments. Some mutual funds invest in stocks, some in bonds, and some in real estate. The mutual fund investor owns shares of the fund, not the actual stocks, bonds, or property purchased by the fund. Most likely, when a person thinks of investing, he or she probably thinks of the stock market. Ownership of a stock represents ownership of a *claim* on the net earnings of a company. Therefore, stock

earnings depend on how well the company is doing. Stocks can be quickly converted to cash by selling them on the stock market, but because the price of stocks changes daily, there is no guarantee that you will get back the money that you paid for the stock. And finally, property or real estate is a popular investment because it can produce returns in two ways: current income and net appreciation (capital gains). You can receive current income if the property is used, such as in situations where tenants are renting it or if crops are grown on the land. Net appreciation occurs if the property increases in value during the time that you own it. A major disadvantage of real estate and rental property is that they are not very liquid; it takes time and resources to turn them into cash. It may take many months to sell a piece of property.

So, which investment will be best for you? Only you can decide. Think carefully about your financial situation, how much money you can or want to invest, and how soon you will need access to the money.

E. Discuss the following questions with a partner.

1. Do you invest your money? If so, how do you invest it?

2. What investment vehicles would you like to try?

3. Would you say you are conservative with your money? Why or why not?

F. **Use the ideas you have learned about investment strategies in this lesson to complete the sentences below. Each sentence may have more than one answer.**

1. If you don't invest your money, you will lose _____ over time.

2. The _____ of stocks is based on the earnings of the company.

3. Savings accounts and mutual funds are not very _____.

4. My favorite investment _____ is _____ (your own idea).

5. It is not easy to _____ real estate into cash.

6. Savings accounts are very _____. You can get the cash whenever you need it.

G. **An outline is a way to organize the main ideas of something you have listened to or read. You can write notes or complete sentences in an outline, but do not directly copy the author's words. Based on the article in Exercise D, complete the outline below.**

I. Inflation

   A. _____

II. Investments make you money.

   A. Current income

   B. _____

   C. _____

III. Popular investment types

   A. _____

   B. _____

   C. Stocks

   D. _____

   E. _____

H. **SUMMARIZE** A summary is a brief statement of main ideas. On a separate piece of paper, write a one-paragraph summary of the article in Exercise D using the notes from your outline in Exercise G.

LESSON 4 Credit

A. **In a small group, discuss the following questions.**

1. What is credit?
2. What makes credit good or bad?
3. How can you find out if you have good or bad credit?
4. If you have bad credit, how can you improve it?

B. **Read the article below. As you read it, underline the main ideas.**

The Four Keys to Great Credit

By Liz Pulliam Weston

Your credit history can make or break you when trying to convince lenders you're a good risk. Here's how to build the best record you can—before you need it:

✓ Open checking and savings accounts. Having bank accounts establishes you as part of the financial mainstream. Lenders want to know you have a checking account available to pay bills, and a savings account indicates you're putting aside something for the future.

✓ Get your credit report—if you have one. Next, you need to find out how lenders view you. Most lenders base their decisions on credit reports, which are compiled by companies known as credit bureaus. You are entitled to a free credit report from each of the three major bureaus each year. Typically, a credit report includes identifying information about you, such as your name, address, social security number, and birth date. The report may also list any credit accounts or loans opened in your name, along with your payment history, account limits, and unpaid balances.

Fix any errors or omissions. Some credit reports include errors— accounts that don't belong to you or that include out-of-date or misleading information. You should read through each of your three reports and note anything that's incorrect. Negative information, such as late payments, delinquencies, liens, and judgments against you, should be dropped after seven years. Bankruptcies can stay on your report for up to ten years.

(continued)

Add positive information to your report. The more information you can provide about yourself, the more comfortable lenders may feel extending credit to you. Here's a list of items to consider:

- Are your employer and your job title listed?
- Is your address listed and correct?
- Is your social security number listed and correct?
- Is your telephone number listed and correct?
- Does your report include all the accounts you've paid on time?

✓ Establish credit. There are three common routes for establishing new credit:

1. Apply for department store and gasoline cards. These are usually easier to get than major bank credit cards.
2. Consider taking out a small personal loan from your local bank or credit union and paying the money back over time. The bank may require you to put up some collateral—such as the same amount you're borrowing, deposited into a savings account.
3. Apply for a secured credit card. These work something like the loan described above: You deposit a certain amount at a bank, and in return you're given a Visa or MasterCard with a credit limit roughly equal to the amount you deposited.

✓ Once you've got credit, use it right. Charge small amounts on each card—but never more than you can pay off each month. You need to use credit regularly to establish your credit history, but there's usually no advantage to paying interest on those charges. Once you've been approved for one card or loan, don't rush out and apply for several more. Applying for too much credit will hurt, rather than help, your score.

C.   ADVISE   Imagine you are a financial advisor. Give your partner advice based on the following questions.

1. What can I do to establish good credit?

   _____

   _____

2. What should I look for in my credit report?

   _____

   _____

3. How can I add positive information to my credit report?

   _____

   _____

D. Go back through the article and underline six words or phrases you do not understand. Work with a partner and look in a dictionary to discover their meanings.

1. _____

2. _____

3. _____

4. _____

5. _____

6. _____

E. On a separate piece of paper, make an outline of the article. Then, write a summary.

F. Having read the article, what are four things you need to do to help establish or maintain your credit?

1. _____
   _____

2. _____
   _____

3. _____
   _____

4. _____
   _____

LESSON **5** Identity theft

GOAL ▪ Protect against identity theft

🎧
CD
TR 12

A. Listen to each of the following people talk about their financial problems. What happened? Take notes on the lines below each photo.

1. _____   2. _____   3. _____

_____   _____   _____

_____   _____   _____

B. Have you ever had any problems similar to the ones in Exercise A? If so, what did you do about it? Tell your classmates.

C. **INFER** In a small group, discuss the following questions.

1. What is identity theft?

2. What do you think the following terms mean: *dumpster diving*, *skimming*, *phishing*, and *pretexting*?

3. What are some things a person who steals your identity might do? Come up with some ideas in addition to the three in Exercise A.

4. What can you do if someone steals your identity?

Protect your PIN when using ATMs.

54 Unit 2

D. Listen to an interview with a member of the Federal Trade Comission (FTC). In each question below, one answer is NOT correct. Circle the incorrect answer.

CD
TR 13

1. What is identity theft?

   a. when someone uses your credit card number without permission to buy things

   b. when someone steals your name and social security number to commit crimes

   c. when someone commits fraud using your personal information

   d. when someone asks you for your personal information

2. What are some ways thieves steal your identity?

   a. dumpster diving

   b. changing your name

   c. stealing

   d. skimming

3. An example of bank fraud is . . .

   a. when someone takes out a loan in your name.

   b. when someone gets a driver's license in your name.

   c. when someone opens an account in your name.

   d. when someone creates counterfeit checks using your account number.

4. How can you find out if your identity has been stolen?

   a. cancel credit card accounts

   b. monitor bank accounts

   c. check credit reports

   d. check bank statements

5. What should you do if your identity has been stolen?

   a. notify creditors

   b. try to find the thief

   c. file a police report

   d. check credit reports

6. How can you help fight identity theft?

   a. donate money to the Federal Trade Commission

   b. be aware of how information is stolen

   c. monitor personal information

   d. educate friends and family about identity theft

E. SUMMARIZE Using the information in Exercise D, work with a group to write a summary about identify theft.

_____

_____

_____

_____

_____

_____

_____

_____

_____

_____

_____

_____

_____

_____

F. In your group, use your summary to prepare a presentation that will educate your classmates about identity theft. Answer the questions below.

1. What information will you present to the class? _____

_____

_____

2. How will you present your information? (orally only, orally and visually, etc.)

_____

3. Who will present which part of the presentation? (Everyone in your group must participate.)

_____

_____

▶ **It's called identity theft**

Before You Watch

A. Look at the picture and answer the questions.

1. Where are Mateo and Naomi?
2. What has happened to Mateo?

While You Watch

B. ▶ **Watch the video and complete the dialog.**

Mr. Sanchez:	… such as your driver's (1) _____license_____ or social security number?
Mateo:	I keep my driver's license and my social (2) _____ card in my wallet.
Mr. Sanchez:	That's all they needed. With that information, they can get into your bank account and take out all your money. They can even start a new account and take out a loan in
	your name. It's called (3) _____ theft.
Mateo:	What (4) _____ I do?
Mr. Sanchez:	Well, the first thing you need to do is (5) _____ your checking account. That will prevent the thieves from taking any more money out of your account.

Check Your Understanding

C. Put the sentences in order to make a conversation.

a. _____ **Customer:** I lost my wallet.

b. _____ **Teller:** What was in it?

c. _____ **Customer:** When can I get a new card?

d. _____ **Teller:** We'd better freeze your account immediately.

e. _____ **Teller:** It'll take about 10 days.

f. _____ **Customer:** My ATM card and my driver's license.

g. _____ **Teller:** What seems to be the problem?

Review

A. Roger and Rupert are brothers who live together. Complete their worksheet below by filling in the missing amounts. Together, Roger and Rupert make $85,000 a year.

MONEY OUT		
	Annual	**Monthly**
Rent	_____	$2,200
Home maintenance fees	_____	$150
Renters' insurance	$1,200	_____
Gas/Electric	_____	$220
Water	_____	$40
Telephone/Cell phone	_____	$120
Food/Restaurants	_____	$400
Medical/Dental	_____	$140
Auto expenses	_____	$890
Clothes/Shoes	$1,125	_____
Hair/Manicure/Facial	_____	$125
Training/Education	$700	_____
Income taxes	$950	_____
Internet	_____	$75
Credit cards/Loans	_____	$975
Entertainment	_____	$425
Cable/Satellite TV	_____	$140
Vacations	$2,500	_____
Gifts	$795	_____
TOTAL		

1. How much do they have left over each year? _____

2. How much do they have left over each month? _____

3. Do you think Roger and Rupert live within their means? _____

4. What suggestions would you make for curbing their spending?

   a. _____

   _____

   b. _____

   _____

   c. _____

   _____

   d. _____

   _____

B. Write four tips for saving money.

1. _____ 2. _____

3. _____ 4. _____

C. Complete each statement with the past perfect continuous and the simple past.

1. Erika _____*had been buying*_____ (buy) lunch every day before she

   _____*started*_____ (start) making it at home.

2. Justin _____ (charge) his credit cards to their maximum limits

   before he _____ (cut) them up.

Learner Log

I can identify investment strategies.	I can maintain good credit.	I can protect against identity theft.
■ Yes ■ No ■ Maybe	■ Yes ■ No ■ Maybe	■ Yes ■ No ■ Maybe

3. Before the Ingrams _____ (buy) a new car, they

_____ (lease) a used one.

4. We _____ (live) beyond our means before we

_____ (organize) our finances.

5. Before she _____ (research) insurance rates, she

_____ (spend) too much on auto insurance.

D. Write four things you have learned about investing on a piece of paper. Share your ideas with a partner. Add two ideas that your partner came up with.

E. Answer the following questions by yourself or with a partner.

1. What is credit? _____

2. What can you do to establish good credit? _____

3. What makes credit good or bad? _____

4. How can you find out if you have good or bad credit? _____

5. If you have bad credit, how can you improve it? _____

6. What should you look for in your credit report? _____

7. How can you add positive information to your credit report? _____

F. Read each scenario. Write what you think happened and what the person should do to fix the problem.

1. Marika tried to withdraw money from her current account, which had over $1,000 in it the last time she checked it, but the bank said she had insufficient funds.

   What happened? _____

   Solution: _____

2. Marco noticed some unfamiliar charges on his credit card statement.

   What happened? _____

   Solution: _____

3. The IRS contacted Frankie and said he never paid income tax on a second job, which he didn't have.

   What happened? _____

   Solution: _____

Vocabulary Review

A. A *synonym* is a word that has the same meaning as another word. Look at each of the words below and choose a word from the box that is its synonym.

bargain	delinquent	fraud
convert	earnings	risk
counterfeit	expense	worth
debt		

1. income _____
2. fake _____
3. late _____
4. scam _____
5. cost _____
6. good deal _____
7. money due _____
8. liability _____
9. change _____
10. value _____

B. Look back in the unit and find three new terms you learned (different from the words in the box in Exercise A). Write a sentence using each of these terms.

1. _____
2. _____
3. _____

C. Complete each sentence with an appropriate word or phrase from this unit. In many cases, more than one word or expression will work.

1. There are many ways in which people can steal your identity. Two of them are

   _____ and _____.

2. A safe way to invest your money is by investing in _____.

3. A riskier way to invest is by investing in _____.

4. One good way to establish credit is _____.

5. Another way is _____.

6. If your identity is stolen, you should _____.

Financial assistance

A. The two agencies below are run by the government and can give people financial assistance. Discuss the questions with your classmates and teacher.

- FDIC (Federal Deposit Insurance Corporation)
  Consumers and Communities

- FTC (Federal Trade Commission)
  Consumer Protection

1. What does the FDIC do? How can they help?

2. What does the FTC do? How can they help?

B. Visit the websites of the agencies in Exercise A to gather more information. Click on the topics you find interesting listed in the consumer section of each site. Write down what you find.

1. fdic.gov: _____

_____

_____

_____

2. ftc.gov: _____

_____

_____

_____

C. Another website that has very useful information for consumers is usa.gov/consumer-complaints. Go to the website and order a free copy of the *Consumer Action Handbook*.

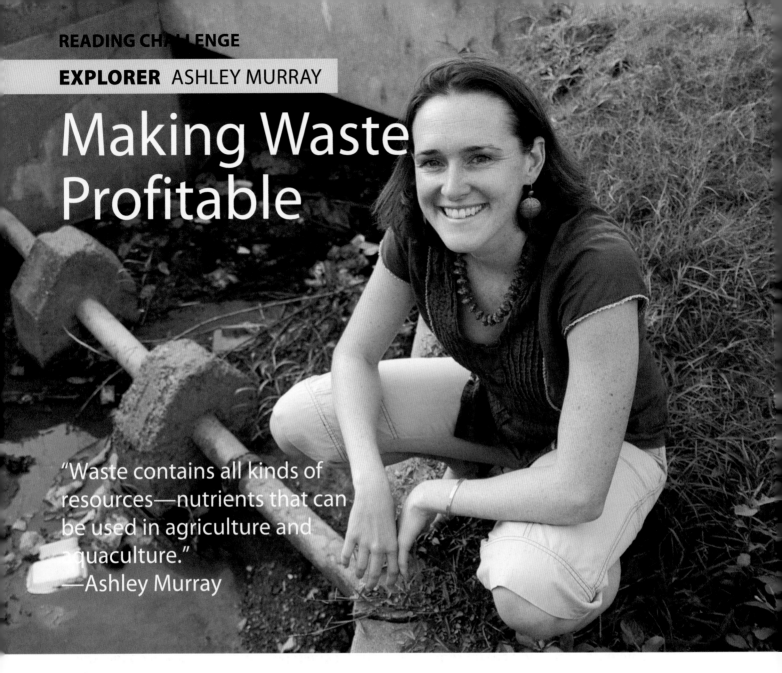

EXPLORER ASHLEY MURRAY

Making Waste Profitable

"Waste contains all kinds of resources—nutrients that can be used in agriculture and aquaculture."
—Ashley Murray

A. PREDICT Read the title and look at the picture. What do you think Ashley Murray's job is?

B. Discuss the questions in a small group.

1. The article you are going to read is about wastewater. What is wastewater and where does the wastewater go in your community?

2. How can wastewater be reused?

3. Do you pay for the wastewater in your community to be reused?

C. Read about Ashley Murray.

What happens to the water that is flushed down our toilets, otherwise known as *wastewater*? In developed countries, the water is treated and can be reused. But in underdeveloped countries, this treatment process is too costly for governments. Ashley Murray is a wastewater engineer who lives in Ghana. She believes, "Any surface water is an open sewage stream. It's hard to overstate the enormous health and environmental impacts of inadequate sanitation." There are over 2.5 billion people in the world with no access to basic sanitation. And "at any given time, half of the hospital beds in the world are filled with people suffering from water-related diseases." And millions of these people die! Ashley wants to solve this problem.

The biggest problem in countries where people have no access to basic sanitation is open sewage drains. This is because the water in those drains has a direct impact on people's health. But the underlying problem is that there is not enough money to do something about it. Households in low-income areas don't have enough money to pay the fees required to treat the waste. And the governments in these countries have more pressing urban challenges than paying to treat the waste. Ashley had to figure out a way to make it an economic benefit for the government to treat and reuse the water.

Ashley set out to prove to the government of Ghana that "waste contains all kinds of resources—nutrients that can be used in agriculture and aquaculture," by starting a company called Waste Enterprises. This company reuses human waste, making things such as fertilizer and fish food. It makes a profit from turning the waste into usable commodities and then puts the profit back into the community to improve sanitation in poor neighborhoods.

Ashley's company is also working with researchers to find other uses for wastewater, such as a replacement for oil. She wants to prove that sanitation can be profitable and not a drain on the government's resources. But "the real goal is improving basic sanitation, health, and environmental conditions for some of the world's poorest populations." If she can do this, she hopes other companies will start doing the same, improving sanitation all around the world.

D. FIND EVIDENCE For each question below, find the answer in the article, underline it, and write the question number next to it.

1. What are the problems with wastewater in developing countries?
2. How is Ashley trying to solve the financial problem?
3. How is she trying to solve the sanitation issue?
4. What can be made with wastewater?

E. Circle the words or phrases in the article that are new to you. Share with a partner and see if you can infer the meanings.

Automotive Know-How

Cars are stored in a tower close to the factory where they are made.

UNIT OUTCOMES

- Purchase a car
- Maintain and repair a car
- Interpret an auto insurance policy
- Compute mileage and gas consumption
- Follow the rules of the road

Look at the photo and answer the questions.

1. What different types of cars can you see?
2. Are the cars new or old? How can you tell?

Vocabulary Builder

A. Look at the different types of cars below. Use the terms in Exercise B to label them.

B. How would you describe each car? Write your ideas next to each term below.

1. two-door coupe: _____

2. four-door sedan: _____

3. convertible: _____

4. minivan: _____

5. sport utility vehicle (SUV): _____

6. sports car: _____

7. station wagon: _____

8. pickup truck: _____

9. van: _____

C. Below are some words and phrases that you will find in this unit. Replace each verb in bold with a synonym from the box. Some words can be used more than once.

change	do	look at
choose	find	replace
commute	imagine	fill up

1. _____ **Change** your air filter.

2. _____ **Check** your oil levels.

3. _____ **Drive** during off-peak hours.

4. _____ **Inspect** your brakes.

5. _____ **Look for** telecommuting opportunities.

6. _____ **Perform** an oil change.

7. _____ **Pick** your lane and stick with it.

8. _____ **Pretend** you have a hybrid.

9. _____ **Replace** your wipers.

10. _____ **Top off** your washer fluid.

D. What do the following words have in common? Write the theme below.

Theme: _____

_____ accident	_____ coverage	_____ make	_____ premium
_____ bodily injury	_____ incident	_____ model	_____ uninsured motorist
_____ collision	_____ limits of liability	_____ policy	_____ VIN

E. **FIND OUT** Check (✓) the terms you know in Exercise D. Circle the ones you don't know. Walk around the classroom and talk to your classmates. Find people who know the terms you have circled.

LESSON ① Buying a car

GOAL ▮ Purchase a car

A. In a group, discuss the following questions.

1. Which type of car do you have? (If you don't have a car, think of someone you know who does.)
2. What is the car like? (Ask about color, size, make, model, etc.)
3. How did you get the car?
4. How long have you had the car?

B. Listen to an auto salesman who is trying to sell you a car. Take notes on what he says about the different types of cars.

CD TR 14

Vehicle	Best for	Pros	Cons
	most people		
			backseats are hard to access
	active family		
		great in good weather	

68　Unit 3

C. IMAGINE You are going to buy a new or used car. Look back at the table in Exercise B. Which type of car would be best for you? Why?

_____

_____

D. GENERATE Now that you have an idea which car is best for you based on the salesman's descriptions, it is a good idea to do some research on your own. What are the best ways to find out more about the car you want to buy? In a group, brainstorm ways to research different car models.

_____

_____

_____

_____

_____

_____

_____

_____

_____

_____

_____

_____

_____

E. Rachel has decided to buy a two-door coupe. Listen and write what she did to research buying her car.

CD
TR 15

1. _____

2. _____

3. _____

4. _____

5. _____

6. _____

F. To supplement your research, ask a variety of people for their opinions about cars. What are some questions you might ask? With a partner, create a list of questions.

Friends and family

1. _____

2. _____

3. _____

Car dealer

1. _____

2. _____

3. _____

Mechanic

1. _____

2. _____

3. _____

Loan officer

1. _____

2. _____

3. _____

G. **CREATE** Make a plan to purchase a car. Write the steps you will take in the plan below.

Step 1: _____

_____

Step 2: _____

_____

Step 3: _____

_____

LESSON ❷ Maintenance and repair

GOAL ▊ Maintain and repair a car

A. With help from your teacher, identify the auto parts below. Write the name of each part in the corresponding box.

air filter	distributor	radiator
alternator	exhaust manifold	rear axle
battery	fuel injection system	rear suspension
brake fluid reservoir	muffler	timing belt
coolant reservoir	power steering reservoir	water pump
disc brake		

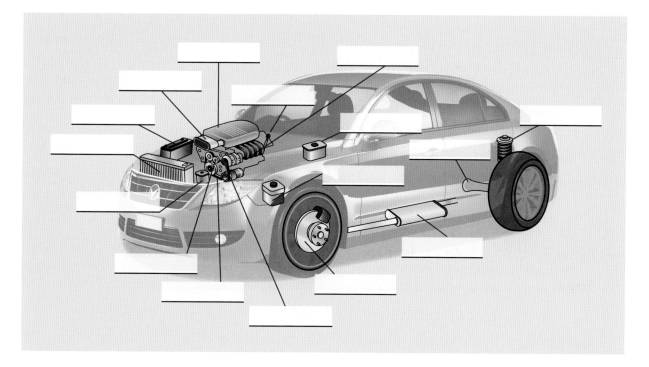

B. **DEFINE** What is the purpose of each auto part in Exercise A? Work with a partner and use a dictionary to define each part on a separate sheet of paper. Share your answers with other pairs.

C. Now that you are more familiar with auto parts and their importance, read this excerpt from an auto maintenance and repair guide.

How to Maintain Your Automobile

Change your air filter. A clogged air filter can affect your gas mileage as well as the performance of your engine. Change it on a regular basis.

Check your oil levels. Your engine needs a certain amount of oil to run properly, so it's important to check the oil levels regularly.

Perform an oil change. As your engine uses oil, the oil becomes dirty and should be changed at regular intervals.

Perform a timing belt inspection. A faulty timing belt can result in bent valves and other expensive engine damage. Check it at least every 10,000 miles, and replace it when the manufacturer recommends doing so.

Replace your wipers. Windshield wipers can wear out, and if they aren't working properly, they could impair your vision while on the road. Change them at least twice a year.

Perform a radiator flush. It's important to keep your radiator and cooling system clean.

Check your power steering fluid. Check your power steering fluid regularly to make sure your power steering doesn't fail.

Inspect your brakes. Protect yourself and your passengers by inspecting your brakes twice a year.

Check and fill your coolant. If your car is low on coolant, it will run hot, so make sure to check the coolant level in your radiator.

Check and replace your spark plugs. A faulty spark plug could cause poor gas mileage and/or a rough running engine and poor acceleration. Make sure to replace the spark plugs as recommended by your car's manual.

Top off your washer fluid. Make sure you have enough washer fluid so you can keep your windshield clean.

Check your wheel bolts. Check the tightness of your wheel bolts on a regular basis to make sure there is no danger of your wheels becoming loose.

D. INTERPRET With a partner, answer the following questions on a separate piece of paper.

1. What fluids need to be regularly checked?

2. Why is it important to replace windshield wipers?

3. Why is it bad to have a clogged air filter?

4. Why should you inspect your timing belt?

5. Why should you check your wheel bolts?

6. What could happen if you don't have enough power steering fluid?

E. Some people can perform their own maintenance while others need the help of trained professionals. Who will do your car repairs? If you need help, how will you find a reliable mechanic? Read the guide below.

Guide to Getting Repairs Done

1. Ask a friend, relative, or coworker for recommendations when looking for a good auto shop or mechanic. Also, take time to find a local garage that you feel comfortable with.
2. Make a list of services you need performed or the symptoms your vehicle is experiencing so there is no misunderstanding.
3. Get more than one opinion about the repairs that need to be done.
4. Ask for a written estimate before the job is started.
5. Get more than one estimate and compare prices.
6. Ask about the warranty policy.
7. Have the mechanic show you what you need replaced and have him or her explain why you need to replace it.
8. Go for a test drive in your car before paying for the repairs. If something is not right with the repairs, make it understood that you are not happy. Do not pay the bill until the vehicle is repaired properly.
9. Pay with a credit card. Many credit cards offer consumer protection for fraud.
10. If you discover something is not fixed after you've paid and driven home, call the garage and explain the situation. Go back to the garage as soon as possible.

F. Take out a piece of paper and write the numbers *1* to *10*. Close your books and see how many suggestions from Exercise E you can remember. Write them down.

G. Make an outline for the guides in Exercises C and E.

H. SUMMARIZE Using your outlines, write a two-paragraph summary of what you have learned in this lesson. Remember to format your paragraphs correctly.

Some people can perform their own maintenance, but it's important to have trained mechanics look at a car.

LESSON ③ Car insurance

GOAL ▨ Interpret an auto insurance policy

A. Discuss these questions with your classmates.

1. Do you drive a car or ride a motorbike?
2. Do you have insurance?
3. Why is it important to have auto insurance?
4. Do you understand your insurance policy?
5. Is it against the law in your state to drive without insurance?

B. Read what each person says about auto insurance policies. Discuss the meanings of the words in italics with a partner.

"An insurance *policy* is a contract between you and the insurance company that states what the company will pay for in the event of an accident." — **Chalene**

"The insurance *premium* is the amount you pay for auto insurance for a certain period of time." — **Keona**

"*Coverage* is what is included in the insurance—what the company will pay for." — **Binata**

C. Look at Chalene's policy and find each of the items below.

★ Bright Star Insurance

Name of Insured and Address: Chalene Johnson 24573 Thatch Street Houston, TX 77042	Policy Number: 05XX 52 870 1625 Q Policy Period: Effective Jan 13, 2017 to Jul 13, 2017
Description of Vehicle(s) Year and Make: 2015 Acurak VIN: QXXPYR18924G23794	Annual Mileage: 9,000 Premium for this Policy Period: $456.40

Coverage	Limits of Liability	Six-Month Premium
A. Bodily Injury	Each Person $100,000; Each Accident $300,000	185.12
B. Collision	Each Accident $50,000	170.81
C. Comprehensive	Each Incident $25,000	44.83
D. Uninsured Motor Vehicle Bodily Injury	Each Person $50,000; Each Accident $150,000	64.64
E. Physical Damage	Deductible $1,000	
		TOTAL $465.40

1. Policy number: _____
2. VIN: _____
3. Policy premium: _____
4. Annual mileage: _____
5. Deductible: _____
6. Make of vehicle: _____

D. There are different types of coverage listed on insurance policies. Match each type of coverage with what it covers. Write the corresponding letters on the lines.

Coverage	What it covers
1. bodily injury liability _____	a. other people's bodily injuries or death for which you are responsible
2. property damage liability _____	b. damage to another vehicle or property
3. collision _____	c. loss or damage to your vehicle or the vehicle you are driving for an incident other than collision (theft, fire, etc.)
4. medical payments _____	d. damage to your vehicle due to an auto accident
5. comprehensive _____	e. bodily injuries to you or your passengers caused by the accident
6. uninsured motorist's bodily injury _____	f. bodily injury caused by another vehicle without insurance
7. uninsured motorist's property damage _____	g. damage caused by another vehicle without insurance

E.   EVALUATE With a partner, read each scenario and decide which coverage would apply.

1. Chalene accidentally ran into a tree and damaged the front end of her car. Which type of

   coverage would apply? _____

2. Binata was driving home from school when she hit another car. She had run through a red light, so the accident was her fault. There was no real damage to her car, but she hurt her back and had to go to the chiropractor. Also, there was significant damage to the car she hit.

   Which types of coverage would apply? _____

3. Keona and his friend Chalene were driving to work when a car hit them from behind. Then, the car drove off without giving them any information. Neither Keona nor Chalene was hurt, but there was damage to Keona's car. Which type of coverage would apply?

   _____

4. Keona's car got stolen from the parking lot at a movie theater. Which type of coverage would

   apply? _____

F. **Look at Chalene's policy in Exercise C. Write a question for each answer.**

EXAMPLE: Chalene Johnson: *Who is being insured through this policy?*

1. $170.81: _____

2. $1,000: _____

3. 05XX 52 870 1625 Q: _____

4. 2015 Acurak: _____

5. $465.40: _____

6. 9,000: _____

G. **Look at Keona's insurance policy and circle the correct answers.**

United Automobile Association • Dallas, TX

STATE: TX
POLICY NUMBER: QQP15 26 49L3798 1
POLICY PERIOD: September 5, 2017 to March 5, 2018
VEHICLE(S): 2012 Fort Ficus, 2008 Chevnoret Tihoe

NAME AND ADDRESS OF INSURED:
Keona lu
54 Plover Plaza
Galveston, TX 50472

Limits of Liability		6-Month Premium
LIABILITY		
Bodily Injury	Each Person $100,000; Each Accident $300,000	98.12
Property Damage	Each Accident $50,000	69.07
UNINSURED MOTORISTS		
Bodily Injury	Each Person $100,000; Each Accident $300,000	27.00
Property Damage	Each Accident $50,000	21.45
PHYSICAL DAMAGE		
Comprehensive Loss	Deductible $1,000	30.92
Collision Loss	Deductible $1,000	96.41
		TOTAL: $342.97

1. How many vehicles are covered by this policy?

   a. 1   b. 2   c. 3   d. 4

2. Where does the insured motorist live?

   a. Dallas   b. Lake Tahoe   c. Galveston   d. Houston

3. How much is United Automobile Association charging for liability?

   a. $98.12   b. $69.07   c. $21.45   d. $167.19

4. What is Keona's deductible for comprehensive loss?

   a. $96.41   b. $30.92   c. $1,000   d. $50,000

LESSON 4 Gas and mileage

GOAL ▮ Compute mileage and gas consumption

🎧 **A.** **Read and listen to the conversation between Keona and Chalene.**

CD
TR 16

Keona: I can't believe the price of gasoline! I've been spending almost $60 just to fill up my tank.

Chalene: Same here. I've been trying to figure out how I can use my car less, so I save some money on gas.

Keona: Any good ideas?

Chalene: Well, I'm going to start carpooling to school two days a week, which should help. And I'm trying to combine my errands, so I only go out once a week.

Keona: That sounds good. I think I'm going to look into public transportation. I have a long drive to work, so maybe I can figure out how to take the train into town. I'll have to drive to the station and park, but at least I won't be driving all the way to work.

Chalene: That's a great idea!

B. **SUGGEST** **Can you think of some other measures Keona and Chalene can take so they won't have to use their cars so much? Write your ideas below.**

_____

_____

C. **Keona wanted to see his gas mileage, so he checked the display in his car. How do you think Keona might calculate his gas mileage in miles per gallon (MPG)? Create a formula and fill in the MPG column in the table.**

Formula: _____				
Date	Odometer	Trip	Gallons	MPG
8/7	12,200	245 miles	13	
8/15	12,475	275	14	
8/24	12,760	285	15	
9/1	13,020	260	14.5	

D. In order to improve your gas mileage, you can follow certain maintenance tips. Listen and write the five tips you hear below.

1. _____

2. _____

3. _____

4. _____

5. _____

E. How will each of the tips in Exercise D help? Listen again and write the reasons on the lines below.

1. _____

2. _____

3. _____

4. _____

5. _____

F. Keona followed the tips. Look at his log below and calculate the MPG and cost per mile. Did his MPG improve?

Date	Odometer	Trip	Gallons	MPG	Cost per gallon	Cost per mile
10/5	14,687	275 miles	13		$3.05	
10/17	14,962	295	14		$3.07	
10/30	15,262	300	15		$2.95	
11/9	15,542	280	14.5		$3.10	

G. **ANALYZE** Look at the cost per mile column in Exercise F. Which week was the cheapest? On a separate piece of paper, write ideas about how Keona can spend less per mile on gas.

H. Here are some tips on how to change your driving habits in order to save money on gas. In a small group, discuss each tip and figure out what it means.

1. Drive the speed limit.

2. Pick your lane and stick with it.

3. Carpool with classmates or coworkers.

4. Don't drive.

5. Drive during off-peak hours.

6. Look for telecommuting opportunities.

I. Keona suggested that Chalene keep track of her gas consumption and mileage. Fill in the missing numbers in her chart below.

Date	Odometer	Trip	Gallons	MPG	Cost per gallon	Cost per mile
10/5	22,758	310	15		$3.10	
10/20		325	16		$3.05	
10/30		320	15.5		$3.12	
11/12		280	17		$2.99	
11/18		275	16.5		$3.03	
AVERAGE						

J. CALCULATE Read about Binata and answer the questions.

1. Binata took a road trip from San Francisco, CA to Salt Lake City, UT. She filled her tank up with gas at $3.75 a gallon and she has an 18-gallon tank. She filled her tank up twice. How much

   did she spend on gas? _____

2. Binata drove 736 miles. How many miles did she get per gallon? _____

3. What was her cost per mile? _____

LESSON ⑤ Traffic laws

A. What does each of the following signs mean? Work with a partner.

_____   _____   _____   _____

_____   _____   _____   _____

_____   _____   _____   _____

_____   _____   _____   _____

B. GENERATE Think about the traffic laws you are familiar with. In a small group, write a law for each item below.

1. yellow light: _You must slow down at a yellow light._

2. speed limit: _____

3. seat belts: _____

4. red light: _____

5. children: _____

6. pedestrians: _____

7. stop sign: _____

8. police officer: _____

9. school bus: _____

C. INTERPRET The United States Department of Transportation has an organization called the National Highway Traffic Safety Administration (NHTSA) whose mission is to "save lives, prevent injuries, and reduce vehicle-related crashes." Read the data from a study the NHTSA conducted and answer the questions that follow.

Seat Belt Use in the States, U.S. Territories, and Nationwide, 2006–2013									
State or U.S. territory	2006	2007	2008	2009	2010	2011	2012	2013	2012–2013 Change
AL	82.9%	82.3%	86.1%	90.0%	91.4%	88.0%	89.5%	97.3%	7.8%
AK	83.2%	82.4%	84.9%	86.1%	86.8%	89.3%	88.1%	86.1%	-2.0%
CA	93.4%	94.6%	95.7%	95.3%	96.2%	96.6%	95.5%	97.4%	1.9%
GA	90.0%	89.0%	89.6%	88.9%	89.6%	93.0%	92.0%	95.5%	3.5%
FL	80.7%	79.1%	81.7%	85.2%	87.4%	88.1%	87.4%	87.2%	-0.2%
IL	87.8%	90.1%	90.5%	91.7%	92.6%	92.9%	93.6%	93.7%	0.1%
MA	66.9%	68.7%	66.8%	73.6%	73.7%	73.2%	72.7%	74.8%	2.1%
NY	83.0%	83.5%	89.1%	88.0%	89.8%	90.5%	90.4%	91.1%	0.7%
TX	90.4%	91.8%	91.2%	92.9%	93.8%	93.7%	94.0%	90.3%	-3.7%
WA	96.3%	96.4%	96.5%	96.4%	97.6%	97.5%	96.9%	94.5%	-2.4%

1. What percentage of drivers wore seat belts in California in 2007? ___94.6%___

2. Where was there a –3.7% difference in seat belt use between 2012 and 2013? _____

3. What percentage of people in Massachusetts wore seat belts in 2013? _____

4. What is the percentage difference in seat belt use between 2012 and 2013 for drivers in Alaska? _____

5. What percentage of drivers wore seat belts in Florida in 2006? _____

D. On a separate piece of paper, write each question above as a statement.

EXAMPLE: *94.6% of drivers in California wore seat belts in 2007.*

E. What are the driving laws regarding alcohol in your state? Discuss them with your class and write them below.

_____

_____

F. Read the facts on alcohol-related accidents. Check (✓) the ones that are the most surprising to you.

☐ Alcohol-related motor vehicle crashes kill someone every 31 minutes and non-fatally injure someone every two minutes.

☐ In 2013, 10,076 people were killed in alcohol-impaired driving crashes, accounting for nearly one-third (31%) of all traffic-related deaths in the United States.

☐ In 2010, over 1.4 million drivers were arrested for driving under the influence of alcohol or narcotics. That's one percent of the 112 million self-reported episodes of alcohol-impaired driving among U.S. adults each year.

☐ Drugs other than alcohol (e.g., marijuana and cocaine) are involved in about 18% of motor vehicle driver deaths. These other drugs are often used in combination with alcohol.

☐ Of the 200 child passengers ages 14 and younger who died in alcohol-impaired driving crashes in 2013, over half (121) were riding in the vehicle with the alcohol-impaired driver.

G. With a partner, rewrite the facts above in your own words.

EXAMPLE: _Someone is killed every half an hour due to a car accident involving alcohol._

H. DECIDE In a small group, make a list of five driving rules that you all think are the most important. Present your list to the class.

1. _____

2. _____

3. _____

4. _____

5. _____

▶ **I wish I had a car**

Before You Watch

A. **Look at the picture and answer the questions.**

1. Where are Mateo, Hector, and Naomi?

2. Where are they going?

While You Watch

B. ▶ **Watch the video and complete the dialog.**

Naomi:	… I can't imagine what the insurance for a car like that would cost. But I guess you wouldn't pay that much for gas. Convertibles get good (1) _____*mileage*_____ .
Mateo:	Who cares about (2) _____ or mileage? The important thing is that you would look good.
Hector:	Personally, I would rather have something more (3) _____, like that pickup.
Mateo:	A (4) _____ ! Are you serious?
Hector:	Think about it. If you got a pickup, you would have lots of (5) _____ in the back.

Check Your Understanding

C. **Write a number next to each quote to show the correct order.**

a. _____ "The mileage on an SUV is terrible."

b. _____ "Convertibles get good mileage."

c. _____ "A pickup? Are you serious?"

d. _____ "Who cares about insurance or mileage?"

e. _____ "I've heard hybrids barely use any gas."

Learner Log

I can purchase a car.
☐ Yes ☐ No ☐ Maybe

I can maintain and repair a car.
☐ Yes ☐ No ☐ Maybe

I can compute mileage and gas consumption.
☐ Yes ☐ No ☐ Maybe

A. List four different types of cars.

1. _____   2. _____

3. _____   4. _____

Which type of car is best for you? _____

B. Recall the auto maintenance tips you learned in Lesson 2. Write the correct verb from the box to complete each tip. You will need to use some of the verbs more than once.

change	check	fill	inspect	perform	replace	top off

1. _____ a radiator flush.

2. _____ your air filter.

3. _____ your washer fluid.

4. _____ your wipers.

5. _____ your power steering fluid.

6. _____ your oil levels.

7. _____ an oil change.

8. _____ a timing belt inspection.

9. _____ your brakes.

10. _____ and _____ your coolant.

11. _____ your wheel bolts.

C. Help Gary calculate his gas mileage and how much he is spending on gas. With a partner, discuss five ways Gary can improve his gas mileage.

Date	Odometer	Trip	Gallons	MPG	Cost per gallon	Cost per mile
2/7	46,269	310	15		$3.02	
2/17		325	16		$2.90	
2/28		320	15.5		$2.95	
3/5		280	17		$3.01	
AVERAGE						

Learner Log

I can interpret an auto insurance policy.	I can follow the rules of the road.
■ Yes ■ No ■ Maybe	■ Yes ■ No ■ Maybe

D. Read the insurance policy and answer the questions on a separate piece of paper.

 DriveRite Automotive Insurance Co., Inc.

Dung Nguyen 79563 Eastern Way Ambrose, GA 31512	Policy Number: QPX2 80 56 45F5542 6 Policy Period: 2/10/15–2/09/16	Vehicle: 2014 Folkswagin Passerine VIN: ZXYI493807T984XXX Annual Mileage: 12,500

Type of Coverage	Cost of Coverage	Limits of Liability
A. Medical	$182.50	Each person $100,000 Each accident $300,000
B. Liability	$175.00	Each person $100,000 Each accident $300,000
C. Collision	$98.26	Each person $50,000 Each accident $50,000
D. Uninsured motorist	$135.00	Each accident $150,000
E. Comprehensive	$76.45	Each incident $25,000

Premium: $667.21

1. Who is being insured through this insurance policy?

2. Where does the insured live?

3. How long is this policy in effect?

4. What is the total premium for the insured's policy?

5. How many miles does the insured drive per year?

6. Dung got in an accident last week, broke his leg, and damaged his car. Which types of coverage will pay for this?

7. How much is the insurance company charging for comprehensive coverage?

8. If the insured's car gets stolen, how much will the insurance company pay to replace the car?

9. What is the most the insurance company will pay for the property damage in an accident?

10. How much will the insurance company pay for each person who is hurt in an accident caused by someone without insurance?

E. On a separate piece of paper, write a summary about one of the topics below.

- Purchasing a car
- Maintaining a car
- Saving money on gas
- Keeping track of gas mileage
- Auto expenditures
- Rules of the road

Vocabulary Review

A. Write the name of each car part below. What does each part do? With a partner, take turns describing each part and its function.

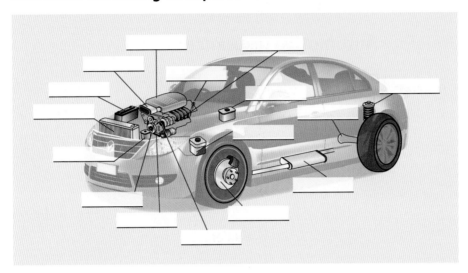

B. Write a defining sentence for each of the words below.

1. coverage: _Coverage is what the insurance company will pay for._

2. premium: _____

3. collision: _____

4. MPG: _____

5. odometer: _____

6. carpool: _____

7. policy: _____

_____

C. Read each phrase below and match it with a vocabulary word or phrase from the unit.

1. restrains driver and/or passengers in an accident: _____seat belt_____

2. identifies your vehicle: _____

3. covers damage to another vehicle: _____

4. can get clogged and affect your gas mileage: _____

5. tells you how fast you can drive on any given road: _____

6. the different things an insurance company will pay for: _____

7. tells you how many miles you have driven: _____

With a team, you will create a section of an auto handbook. With the class, you will compile sections into a complete auto handbook.

1. **COLLABORATE** Form a team with four or five students. Choose positions for each member of your team.

Position	Job description	Student name
Student 1: Project Leader	Check that everyone speaks English. Check that everyone participates.	
Student 2: Secretary	Take notes on team's ideas.	
Student 3: Designer	Design layout of handbook section.	
Student 4: Spokesperson	Prepare team for presentation.	
Student 5: Assistant	Help secretary and designer with their work.	

2. As a class, brainstorm a list of topics to include in your auto handbook. You might include maintenance tips, directions on reading an insurance policy, and rules of the road. Count the number of teams and narrow your list of topics down to that number. Each team must choose a single topic to work on.

3. As a team, gather all the information for your group's section of the handbook.

4. Decide how you would like to present your information. You can choose pictures, lists of facts, and graphs. Be creative!

5. Create your section of the handbook.

6. Present your section of the handbook to the class.

7. Compile all the sections into one handbook.

EXPLORER YU-GUO GUO

Fully Charged

"There is a serious need for sustainable energy sources to power electrical devices."
—Yu-Guo Guo

A. **PREDICT** Look at the title and read the quote. What job do you think Yu-Guo Guo has?

B. Batteries allow us to use things without having to plug them in. Make a list of things that use batteries.

1. _____   2. _____
3. _____   4. _____
5. _____   6. _____
7. _____   8. _____

C. Discuss the following questions in a small group.

1. Do you drive a car? Why?

2. Do you think cars are bad for the environment? Why?

D. Yu-Guo Guo is a chemist who has been working with nanotechnology to change the way cars are made. Read the interview.

Q: Why is there a need for electric vehicles (EVs)?

Yu-Guo Guo: There is a serious need for sustainable energy sources to power electrical devices, cars being one of them. Traditional sources, such as fossil fuels, cannot satisfy the growing demand, and the carbon emissions that cars give off raise great environmental concerns.

Q: If that is the case, why don't more people drive EVs?

Yu-Guo Guo: EVs are expensive because of the battery pack—the most important part of any EV. Batteries that are powerful enough to make cars go long distances are big and heavy, which makes an EV too costly for most consumers. On the other hand, using a smaller battery pack means the car couldn't go as far, making them undesirable for most drivers.

Q: So is there a feasible solution?

Yu-Guo Guo: The key to improving performance and lowering the battery cost is using nanoparticles that can quickly absorb and hold many lithium ions. This will improve the performance without causing deterioration in the electrode. In plain terms, this means that cars won't drain the energy storage capacity quickly. Compared with traditional lithium-ion batteries, this new high-power technology means batteries can be fully charged in just a few minutes, as quickly and easily as you fill your car with gas. These advanced batteries recover more energy when cars stop, deliver more power when cars start, and enable vehicles to run longer.

Q: Why hasn't this been done before?

Yu-Guo Guo: I invented the technology, so it hasn't been possible before. I found a unique way to make an important part of this technology—lithium iron phosphate—less expensive and easier for manufacturers to work with.

Q: How soon will we start to see the EVs with the better, smaller battery packs?

Yu-Guo Guo: Five years from now, the electric vehicle market should be well established. In cities, up to 10 percent of cars could be EVs.

E. Based on the interview, match each vocabulary expression to its correct meaning.

1. sustainable	a. rechargeable power source
2. lithium-ion battery	b. microscopic particle of matter
3. deterioration	c. not wanted or wished for
4. nanoparticle	d. fuel formed from the remains of living organisms
5. fossil fuels	e. able to be maintained at a certain rate or level
6. undesirable	f. process of becoming progressively worse

F. **INFER** Underline any words or phrases in the article that you don't understand and try to infer the meanings.

Housing

A modern apartment block is illuminated by residents' lights at night.

UNIT OUTCOMES

- Communicate issues by phone
- Interpret rental agreements
- Identify tenant and landlord rights
- Get insurance
- Prevent theft

Look at the photo and answer the questions.

1. What type of housing can you see?
2. What can the tenants in this type of housing do to prevent theft?

Vocabulary Builder

A. **What do the following words have in common? Write the theme below.**

abandon	dwelling	grounds	summon
burglarize	enticing	premises	theft
crime	evident	responsible	thief
disturbance	exterior	seize	weapons

Theme: _____

B. **CLASSIFY** **Put each word in the correct column according to its part of speech. Use a dictionary if you need help.**

Noun	Verb	Adjective

C. **Choose two words from each column in Exercise B. Write one sentence using each word.**

1. _____

2. _____

3. _____

4. _____

5. _____

6. _____

D. Read.

You can often identify a word's part of speech just by looking at it. The following words are nouns. What do they have in common?

prevention   installation   expiration

The roots of these words are verbs: *prevent, install,* and *expire.* The suffix *-(a)tion* changes each verb into a noun. The noun form signifies the action or process of doing the action. For example, *prevention* signifies the action of preventing something.

E. Change each verb below into its noun form. Then, define each new word on a separate piece of paper. Use a dictionary to check your spelling.

1. activate   _____

2. compensate   _____

3. deteriorate   _____

4. estimate   _____

5. litigate   _____

6. possess   _____

7. terminate   _____

8. vacate   _____

F. DETERMINE Without using a dictionary, match the phrases with their definitions.

_____ 1. fit for human occupancy	a. advance warning written in a business letter
_____ 2. formal written notice	b. estimate of how much one might pay for insurance
_____ 3. full compliance	c. being gone for a long time; longer than expected
_____ 4. housing codes	d. built well; building in good condition
_____ 5. insurance quote	e. doing what one is required to do
_____ 6. prolonged absence	f. government regulations for building houses
_____ 7. replacement cost	g. government rules regarding health and cleanliness
_____ 8. sanitary regulations	h. suitable for people to live in
_____ 9. structurally sound	i. taking up a lot of time
_____ 10. time-consuming	j. cost of replacing something

LESSON ❶ I have a problem

🎧 **A. Read and listen to the phone conversation Ming Mei is having with her landlord.**
What is the problem? How is the landlord going to fix it?

CD
TR 18

Landlord:	Hello?
Ming Mei:	Hi, Mr. Martin. This is Ming Mei from the apartment on Spring Street.
Landlord:	Oh, hi, Ming Mei. What's up? Is there a problem?
Ming Mei:	Well, after all the rain we had this weekend, the roof has started leaking. I think there may be a pool of water still on the roof because water is leaking through our ceiling even though the rain has stopped.
Landlord:	Oh, no. Has it damaged the carpet?
Ming Mei:	No, we caught it right away and put a bucket down to collect the drips.
Landlord:	Oh, great. Thanks for being on top of it. I'll have my handyman come over and look at the roof and your ceiling. Can you let him in around ten this morning?
Ming Mei:	I have to go to work, but I can get my sister to come over.
Landlord:	Great. Thanks for calling, Ming Mei.
Ming Mei:	Thank you, Mr. Martin.

B. Practice the conversation with a partner. Switch roles.

🎧 **C. Listen to the conversations between tenants and landlords. Take notes in the**
table below.

CD
TR 19–21

	Problem	Solution
Conversation 1		
Conversation 2		
Conversation 3		

In a rented home, the landlord is responsible for maintenance.

D. **INTERPRET** Look at the following statements from the conversation between Ming Mei and her landlord in Exercise A. Answer the questions.

I'll have my handyman come over and look at the roof and your ceiling.

1. Who is the subject of the sentence? _____

2. Who is going to come over? _____

… I can get my sister to come over.

3. Who is the subject of the sentence? _____

4. Who is going to come over? _____

E. We use causative verb structures when we want to indicate that the subject causes something to happen. Study the chart with your teacher.

Causative Verbs: *Get, Have, Help, Make, Let*			
Subject	**Verb**	**Noun/Pronoun**	**Infinitive (Omit *to* except with *get*.)**
He	will get	his handyman	to come.
She	had	her mom	wait for the repairperson.
The landlord	helped	me	move in.
Ming Mei	makes	her sister	pay half of the rent.
Mr. Martin	let	Ming Mei	skip one month's rent.

F. Match each causative verb from Exercise E with its meaning. Two verbs have the same meaning.

_____ 1. get   a. allow

_____ 2. have   b. provide assistance

_____ 3. help   c. delegate responsibility to someone

_____ 4. let   d. require

_____ 5. make

G. Unscramble the words and phrases to make causative statements. Then, write housing-related sentences of your own using the same verbs.

1. them / had / their landlord / and leave a deposit / fill out an application

   Their landlord had them fill out an application and leave a deposit.

   My wife had me paint the children's bedroom.

2. to prospective renters / him / let / the apartment / show / his tenants

   _____

   _____

3. made / my parents / a condo / buy / me

   _____

   _____

4. my boss / for me / will get / I / to write / a letter of reference

   _____

   _____

5. her husband / she / which house to rent / decide / will let

   _____

   _____

6. find / my cousin / me / a new place to live / helped

   _____

   _____

H. What should you do when you call your landlord? Read the sentences below and put them in the correct order (1–4).

_____ Restate the solution for clarification.   _____ Ask for a solution.

_____ Clearly identify the problem.   _____ State your name and where you live.

I. **GENERATE** What are some problems you might have with your home that would require you to call your landlord? Brainstorm a list on a separate piece of paper with a partner.

J. With a partner, practice having phone conversations with a landlord. Follow the order of events from Exercise H and describe some of the problems you brainstormed in Exercise I.

LESSON ❷ Understand the fine print

A. Have you ever rented a property? If so, do you remember the information that was in your rental agreement? Make a list on a separate piece of paper.

B. Rental agreements are long and contain information to protect the tenant and the landlord. Much of the agreement is about money. Read the money-related section of a rental agreement.

> RENT: To pay as rental the sum of $ _____ per month, due and payable in advance from the first day of every month. Failure to pay rent when due will result in the Owner taking immediate legal action to evict the Resident from the premises and seize the security deposit.
>
> LATE FEE: Rent received after the first of the month will be subject to a late fee of 10% plus $3.00 per day.
>
> SECURITY DEPOSIT: Resident agrees to pay a deposit in the amount of $ _____ to secure Resident's pledge of full compliance with the terms of this agreement. The security deposit will be used at the end of the tenancy to compensate the Owner for any damages or unpaid rent or charges. Further damages will be repaired at Resident's expense with funds other than the deposit.
>
> RETURN OF DEPOSIT: Security deposits will be deposited for the Resident's benefit in a non-interest-bearing bank account. Release of these deposits is subject to the provisions of State Statutes and as follows:
>
> A. The full term of this agreement has been completed.
>
> B. Formal written notice has been given.
>
> C. No damage or deterioration to the premises, building(s), or grounds is evident.
>
> D. The entire dwelling, appliances, closets, and cupboards are clean and left free of insects; the refrigerator is defrosted; all debris and rubbish has been removed from the property; and the carpets are cleaned and left odorless.
>
> E. Any and all unpaid charges, pet charges, late charges, extra visitor charges, delinquent rents, utility charges, etc., have been paid in full.
>
> F. All keys have been returned, including keys to any new locks installed while Resident was in possession.
>
> G. A forwarding address has been left with the Owner.
>
> Thirty days after termination of occupancy, the Owner will send the balance of the deposit to the address provided by the Resident, payable to the signatories hereto, or the Owner will impose a claim on the deposit and so notify the Resident by certified letter. If such written claim is not sent, the Owner relinquishes the right to make any further claim on the deposit and must return it to the Resident provided Resident has given the Owner notice of intent to vacate, abandon, and terminate this agreement prior to the expiration of its full term, at least seven days in advance.

C. **ANALYZE** In a group, interpret the money portion of the rental agreement. Underline words or phrases no one in your group understands and ask your teacher.

D. Read the sections on maintenance and repairs.

MAINTENANCE: Resident agrees to maintain the premises during the period of this agreement. This includes woodwork, floors, walls, furnishings and fixtures, appliances, windows, screen doors, lawns, landscaping, fences, plumbing, electrical, air-conditioning and heating, and mechanical systems. Tacks, nails, or other hangers nailed or screwed into the walls or ceilings will be removed at the termination of this agreement. Damage caused by rain, hail, or wind as a result of leaving windows or doors open, or damage caused by overflow of water, or stoppage of waste pipes, breakage of glass, damage to screens, deterioration of lawns and landscaping—whether caused by abuse or neglect—is the responsibility of the Resident.

RESIDENT'S OBLIGATIONS: The Resident agrees to meet all Resident's obligations including:

A. Taking affirmative action to ensure that nothing exists that might place the Owner in violation of applicable building, housing, and health codes.

B. Keeping the dwelling clean and sanitary; removing garbage and trash as they accumulate; maintaining plumbing in good working order to prevent stoppages and/or leakage of plumbing, fixtures, faucets, pipes, etc.

C. Operating all electrical, plumbing, sanitary, heating, ventilating, a/c, and other appliances in a reasonable and safe manner.

D. Assuring that property belonging to the Owner is safeguarded against damage, destruction, loss, removal, or theft.

REPAIRS: In the event repairs are needed beyond the competence of the Resident, he or she is urged to arrange for professional assistance. Residents are offered the discount as an incentive to make their own decisions on the property they live in. Therefore, as much as possible, the Resident should refrain from contacting the Owner except for emergencies or for repairs costing more than the discount since such involvement by the Owner will result in the loss of the discount. ANY REPAIR THAT WILL COST MORE THAN THE AMOUNT OF THE DISCOUNT MUST BE APPROVED BY THE OWNER OR THE TENANT WILL BE RESPONSIBLE FOR THE ENTIRE COST OF THAT REPAIR. Any improvement made by the tenant shall become the property of the Owner at the conclusion of this agreement.

E. Divide into two groups and present. One group will present the responsibilities for maintenance, and the other group will present the responsibilities for repairs.

F. SUMMARIZE Make a summary of your section for the class.

G. Based on what you have read so far, what do you think the rental agreement will say about each of the following items? Write your ideas.

Lead-based paint: _____

Phone: _____

Smoke detectors: _____

Utilities: _____

H. Read the information taken from the rental agreement about the topics in Exercise G. Write the correct topic on the line that follows each section.

1. Resident agrees to install and maintain telephone service and agrees to furnish to the Owner the phone number, and any changes, within 3 days after installation.

   _____

2. Smoke detectors have been installed in this residence. It's the Resident's responsibility to maintain appliances including testing periodically and replacing batteries as recommended by the manufacturer. In the event the detectors are missing or inoperative, the tenant has an affirmative duty to notify the landlord immediately.

   _____

3. Resident shall be responsible for payments of all utilities, garbage, water and sewer charges, telephone, gas, or other bills incurred during his/her residency. He/She specifically authorizes the Owner to deduct amounts of unpaid bills from their deposits in the event they remain unpaid after the termination of this agreement.

   _____

4. Houses built before 1978 may contain lead-based paint. Lead from paint, paint chips, and dust can pose health hazards if not taken care of properly. Lead exposure is especially harmful to young children and pregnant women. Before renting pre-1978 housing, Owner must disclose the presence of known lead-based paint and lead-based paint hazards in the dwelling. Resident must also receive a federally approved pamphlet of lead-poisoning prevention.

   _____

I. **SUMMARIZE** With a partner, go back through the sections of the rental agreement in this lesson. Make a list of all the topics. Then, on a separate piece of paper, write a statement about each topic, summarizing what the rental agreement says about it.

LESSON ③ Your rights

GOAL ▮ Identify tenant and landlord rights

A. Discuss the following terms with a partner. Define them with your teacher.

1. What is a *right*?

   _____

2. What is a *responsibility*?

   _____

B. Tenants have rights and responsibilities, just as landlords do. Read the list below and indicate which responsibility belongs to each person: tenant (*T*) or landlord (*L*).

1. _____ Provide a clean apartment when the tenant moves in.

2. _____ Maintain common areas (hallways, stairs, yards, entryways).

3. _____ Give the landlord permission to enter the apartment at reasonable times and with advance notice to inspect it or to make any necessary repairs.

4. _____ Keep noise at a level that will not disturb neighbors.

5. _____ Keep the apartment and the surrounding area clean and in good condition.

6. _____ Notify the landlord immediately if the apartment needs repair through no fault of the tenant.

7. _____ Notify the landlord of any anticipated prolonged absence from the apartment so he or she can keep an eye on things.

8. _____ Pay the rent on time.

9. _____ Provide properly working plumbing and heating (both hot and cold running water).

10. _____ Repair any damage occurring to the apartment through the fault of the tenant, tenant's family members, or tenant's guests. Notify landlord at once of major damage.

11. _____ Provide well-lit hallways and entryways.

12. _____ When moving out, give landlord proper advance notice. Be sure that the apartment is in the same condition as when the tenant moved in and return the key to the landlord promptly.

C. RESTATE With a partner, restate each of the rights and responsibilities in Exercise B.

EXAMPLE: "It is a landlord's responsibility to provide a clean apartment when the tenant moves in."

D. Read about the implied warranty of habitability.

The *implied warranty of habitability* states that a landlord must keep the property in a condition fit for human occupancy. In other words, it must be a safe place for human beings to live. Here are some questions a landlord might ask him or herself before renting a property: Are there any known hazards with the property? Do the fixtures work properly? Is the building structurally sound? Does the property have any recurring problems?

If a landlord does not comply with the *implied warranty of habitability*, a tenant can cancel the lease, leave the premises, take the costs of repairs out of the rent, or ask for monetary damages.

In determining whether a landlord has violated the *implied warranty of habitability*, courts will look at several factors:

1. Is the problem violating a housing code?
2. Is the problem violating a sanitary regulation?
3. Is the problem affecting a needed facility?
4. How long has the problem lasted?
5. How old is the building?
6. How much is the rent?
7. Has the tenant been ignoring the problem?
8. Is the tenant in any way responsible for the problem?

One or more of these factors will help the courts determine who is at fault and what the victim's rights may be.

E. ANALYZE In a small group, discuss the following questions.

1. If your landlord violated the implied warranty of habitability, what can you do?

_____

_____

2. According to the list of questions that courts will ask, what are some situations in which you could take a landlord to court?

_____

_____

3. What are some situations when you couldn't take a landlord to court?

_____

_____

F. DETERMINE With a partner, look at each picture below. Decide if it violates the *implied warranty of habitability*. Imagine that each of these situations has gone on for at least three weeks with no response from the landlord.

G. Imagine that you are a landlord. Use the rights and responsibilities in Exercise B to write statements using a causative verb structure.

1. The law makes me provide a clean apartment for the tenant when he or she moves in.

2. _____

3. _____

4. _____

5. _____

H. Imagine that you are a tenant. Use the rights and responsibilities in Exercise B to write statements using a causative verb structure.

1. The law makes me pay the rent on time.

2. _____

3. _____

4. _____

5. _____

GOAL ▪ Get insurance

🎧
CD
TR 22

A. Discuss the terms of the insurance quote below. Then, listen to Makela and Bryce talk about it.

Renter's Insurance Quote	
Value of personal property	$29,000
Deductible	$250
Liability	$100,000
Medical payments	$1,000
Annual premium	$220.08
Monthly payment	$18.34

B. Discuss the following questions with your classmates.

1. Do you have insurance for your property? Why or why not?

2. What is a deductible? What is Makela's deductible?

3. What is the liability insurance for?

4. What are the medical payments for?

5. How much will Makela pay for one year of renter's insurance?

C. EVALUATE What is the value of your personal property? Write the estimated replacement costs below.

Personal property	Typical replacement cost	Your estimated replacement cost
Personal computer, accessories, and software	$1,500–$4,000	
TV and stereo equipment (home and portable)	$500–$4,000	
Music and movie collection	$500–$2,000	
Furniture and household items	$5,000–$15,000	
Clothing and shoes	$2,000–$4,000	
Sporting goods	$500–$2,000	
Camera and video equipment	$200–$1,000	
Jewelry and watches	$1,000	
Other (luggage, tools, etc.)	$1,000–$3,000	
Total estimated replacement costs		

D. **CONTRAST** Landlords should carry insurance for the structures they rent to others. How do you think homeowner's insurance is different from renter's insurance?

E. Read the Hahns' homeowner's insurance policy below. Then, answer the questions that follow.

State One Insurance

Name/Address of Insured: Steve and Rosemary Hahn 7930 Inca Way Kansas City, MO 64108	
Deductible: $2,500	Annual Premium: $1,077.93
Coverage Type	**Amount of Coverage**
Dwelling	$401,000
Personal Property	$300,750
Loss of Use	$80,200
Personal Liability—Each Occurrence	$100,000
Medical Payments to Others—Each Person	$1,000

1. How much will the insurance company pay to rebuild the house? _____

2. How much will the insurance company pay to replace personal belongings? _____

3. How much will the family have to pay before the insurance company pays? _____

4. What is the monthly premium? _____

F. To get homeowner's insurance, the insurance company needs information about your building. Read about the Hahns' home. Then, fill in the information about your home.

Building feature	Hahns' home	My home
Year built	1986	
Total square footage	2,378 sq. ft.	
Number of stories	2	
Exterior wall construction material	stucco on frame	
Roof type	clay tile	
Garage or carport	attached garage: 2-car	
Wall partitions construction materials	drywall	
Wall/Floor covering materials	paint/wood and tile	
Number of kitchens/bathrooms	1/3	
Type of air/heat	central air/gas	

G. Do you have insurance? Answer the questions that apply to you.

I have insurance.

1. What type of policy do you have? (homeowner's, renter's) _____

2. How long have you had your policy? _____

3. What is your monthly premium? _____

4. How often do you review your policy in case changes need to be made?

    _____

I don't have insurance.

1. What type of policy do you need? (homeowner's, renter's) _____

2. How can you find an insurance company? _____

    _____

3. How much personal property coverage do you need? _____

    _____

4. How much can you spend per month on insurance? ($50, $100, $150) _____

H. Using the questions in Exercise G, interview three classmates and take notes.

Name: _____ Insurance (yes/no) Type: _____

Notes: _____

Name: _____ Insurance (yes/no) Type: _____

Notes: _____

Name: _____ Insurance (yes/no) Type: _____

Notes: _____

I. **PLAN** On a separate piece of paper, write a statement about what you are going to do to protect your home and personal property.

EXAMPLE: *I need renter's insurance for my personal property. This week, I'm going to go online and get quotes from three insurance companies.*

LESSON **5** Protecting your home

A. Use a dictionary to define the two sets of words below. Include the part of speech for each word. Then, answer the questions that follow.

burglar: _____

burglarize/burgle: _____

burglary: _____

theft: _____

thief: _____

thieve: _____

1. What is the difference between the two sets of words? _____

   _____

2. There are three pairs of synonyms in the groups of words above. Write them on a separate piece of paper.

B. **PREDICT** You are about to read a newsletter on how to protect your home from being burglarized. What do you think it will say about the following items? Brainstorm with a group.

Light	Time	Noise

Security lights help to deter burglars.

C. Read the newsletter.

Theft Prevention Newsletter

Burglary Prevention

Each year in the United States, there are more than five million home burglaries. Nine out of ten of these crimes are preventable. The risk of being burglarized can be greatly reduced by taking simple steps to make your home more difficult to enter and less enticing to would-be burglars. **Remember the greatest weapons in the fight to prevent burglaries are light, time, and noise.**

Light

- ○ Make sure that exterior lights are mounted out of reach so that burglars can't easily unscrew bulbs.
- ○ Consider buying motion-sensitive lights, which are now available at relatively low prices.
- ○ Use a variable light timer to activate lights inside your home.
- ○ Trim trees and shrubs near doors and windows so burglars can't hide in the shadows.

Time

Make it time-consuming for a burglar to break into your home by ...
- ○ installing deadbolt locks on all exterior doors.
- ○ installing double key locks in doors that contain glass. This will keep a burglar from being able to open the door simply by breaking the glass and reaching through.
    (Note: So that everyone in the house can get out in the event of a fire, be sure to keep the key in a designated place.)
- ○ placing additional locks on all windows and patio doors.

Noise

- ○ Get a dog. You don't need a large attack dog; even a small dog creates a disturbance that burglars would prefer to avoid. Remember to license and vaccinate it.
- ○ Consider having someone care for your dogs in your home while you're away instead of boarding them.
- ○ If you can afford it, install an alarm system that will alert neighbors of a burglar's presence. Most systems can even summon local police directly.

D. **COMPARE** Look at the ideas you brainstormed in Exercise B and the tips from the newsletter. Are there any tips you didn't think of? List them in the table.

Light	Time	Noise

🎧 **E.** Listen to the police officer talk about other tips to prevent a break in. Write the tips below.

CD
TR 23

1. _____

2. _____

3. _____

4. _____

5. _____

6. _____

🎧 **F.** Sometimes all your efforts will not stop a determined burglar. It is wise to take some precautions that will help you get your property back should a criminal successfully break into your home. Listen to the police officer and take notes.

CD
TR 24

1. _____

2. _____

3. _____

4. _____

5. _____

6. _____

G. **CREATE** Make a flier to post in your community. Include the most important tips you learned about how to prevent theft in your home.

Some communities form Neighborhood Watch groups to look out for each other.

NEIGHBORHOOD WATCH

PROGRAM IN FORCE

We report all Suspicious Persons & Activities to our Enforcement Agency

LIFESKILLS ▶ I'll have my handyman fix it

Before You Watch

A. Look at the picture and answer the questions.

1. What problem do Hector, Mateo, and Naomi have?

2. Who is the man in the blue shirt?

While You Watch

B. ▶ Watch the video and complete the dialog.

Hector: Yeah, the ceiling is still (1) ___*dripping*___ even though the rain has stopped.

Landlord: I see. Has the water (2) _____ the floor?

Naomi: No, we caught it right away and put a bucket down to collect all the

(3) _____ .

Hector: But we can't keep emptying out this (4) _____ day and night. And, the damage to the ceiling is getting worse.

Mateo: That's right. And we can't be (5) _____ for any damage if the water spills over.

Landlord: I'll have my (6) _____ come by tomorrow morning. Can one of you be here to let him in?

Check Your Understanding

C. Write a number next to each quote to show the correct order.

a. _____ **Landlord:** I'll have it repaired tomorrow.

b. _____ **Tenant:** Thank you. I appreciate it.

c. _____ **Landlord:** I got your message. What's the matter?

d. _____ **Tenant:** Can you fix it sooner than that? It's very cold.

e. _____ **Landlord:** In that case, I'll fix it today.

f. _____ **Tenant:** My heater stopped working yesterday.

g. _____ **Landlord:** You're welcome. Sorry for the inconvenience.

Review

Learner Log

I can communicate issues by phone.
■ Yes ■ No ■ Maybe

I can interpret rental agreements.
■ Yes ■ No ■ Maybe

A. With a partner, practice conversations between a tenant and a landlord. Practice both face-to-face and phone conversations. Use the scenarios below.

1. leaky faucet
2. broken window
3. can't pay rent on time
4. noisy neighbors

B. Using the words provided below, write complete sentences using the causative verb structure. You may choose the verb tense to use.

1. she / make / her sister / move

   She made her sister move out of her apartment.

2. I / get / her / meet

3. they / have / their friends / wait

4. Elliot / help / his father / repair

5. my father / make / me / pay

6. his landlord / let / him / fix

C. Make a list of topics that can be found in a rental agreement. After each topic, write a typical statement that might be found in such an agreement.

1. *Rent: The rent must be paid on the first day of each month.*

2.

3.

4.

5.

6.

Learner Log

I can identify tenant and landlord rights.   I can get insurance.   I can prevent theft.
■ Yes   ■ No   ■ Maybe   ■ Yes   ■ No   ■ Maybe   ■ Yes   ■ No   ■ Maybe

D. Identify one right for tenants and one right for landlords.

1. A tenant has the right to _____.

2. A landlord has the right to _____.

E. Read the insurance policy and answer the questions.

Insurance Policy

Deductible: $2,250.00	Annual Premium: $989.45
Coverage Type	**Amount of Coverage**
Dwelling	$330,000
Loss of Use	$80,200
Medical Payments to Others—Each Person	$1,000
Personal Liability—Each Occurrence	$100,000
Personal Property	$200,000

1. Is this a homeowner's or renter's policy? _____

   How do you know? _____

2. How much will the insurance company pay to rebuild the house? _____

3. What is the annual premium? _____

4. How much will the insurance company pay to replace personal belongings? _____

F. Write _T_ (true) or _F_ (false) in front of each theft prevention tip.

_____ 1. Place your valuables in easy-to-see locations.

_____ 2. Lock up anything that could be used to break into your home.

_____ 3. Install an alarm system.

_____ 4. Make sure you turn off all the lights when you leave your home.

_____ 5. Install double key locks on all your windows.

_____ 6. Let your neighbors know when you will be out of town.

Vocabulary Review

A. Complete each question with a word or phrase from this unit. There may be more than one correct answer.

1. Are you a tenant or a _____?

2. How much _____ do you have for your personal property?

3. Do you have _____ or _____ insurance?

4. What is your monthly _____?

5. Do you have an _____ installed in your house?

6. What would your landlord do if there were a _____ in your building?

B. With a partner, ask and answer the questions in Exercise A.

C. Without using a dictionary, define the following words. Include the part of speech.

1. dwelling: _____

2. policy: _____

3. right: _____

4. burglary: _____

5. responsibility: _____

6. prevent: _____

7. vacate: _____

8. premium: _____

D. With a partner, write a conversation using as many of the words from Exercise C as you can include.

Student A: _____

Student B: _____

Student A: _____

Student B: _____

Student A: _____

Student B: _____

Student A: _____

Student B: _____

Presentation Topics

- Communication with a landlord or tenant
- Rental agreements
- Tenant and landlord rights
- Renter's or homeowner's insurance
- Theft prevention

1. **COLLABORATE** Form a team with four or five students. Decide which topic your team will work on. (Each team should choose a different topic from the list above.)

2. Choose positions for each member of your team.

Position	Job description	Student name
Student 1: Project Leader	Check that everyone speaks English. Check that everyone participates.	
Student 2: Project Secretary	Take notes on your team's ideas.	
Student 3: Coordinator	Divide presentation into parts. Assign each team member one part of the presentation.	
Student 4: Director	Organize a different method of presentation for each part.	
Student 5: Advisor	Give feedback on the presentation as each team member rehearses his/her part.	

3. Gather the information for your presentation.

4. Decide how to present your information to the class. For example, you may want to use charts, role plays, or games.

5. Create any materials needed for your presentation.

6. Rehearse your presentation.

7. Give your presentation to the class.

EXPLORER CONSTANCE ADAMS

Out of This World

"We need to understand how our planet and all the little systems inside of it can coexist without causing too much strain. I'd like to find a way to bring it all back home again."
—Constance Adams

A. PREDICT Answer the questions about the small picture.

1. What type of housing do you think this is?
2. What makes it different from typical housing?
3. How is it the same?

B. Match the following words to their correct meanings.

1. coexist
2. fluctuation
3. inflatable
4. launch
5. requirements
6. strain
7. terrestrial
8. withstand

a. irregular rising and falling of something
b. remain undamaged or unaffected by
c. things that are needed or wanted
d. live at the same time or in the same place
e. ability to be filled with air
f. relating to the earth
g. excessive demand on the strength of something
h. send into outer space

C. Read about Constance Adams.

What if your job was to design a house for space? Well, this was one of the first projects that NASA gave to Constance Adams, a space architect. Space housing cannot be like housing you would find on Earth. There are certain requirements: It would have to "withstand phenomenal strain, radiation, up to 500 degrees of temperature fluctuation, and orbital debris moving faster than a high-speed bullet—with an inflatable shell." And one more thing: It can only be 14 feet in diameter for a launch, but once it gets to space, it needs to expand to three times that size.

In the 1990s, NASA (National Aeronautics and Space Administration) started working on a concept for a transit habitat for the very first human mission to Mars. It was called TransHab (Transit Habitat). Aerospace company Lockheed Martin hired Constance, who studied sociology at Harvard University and a master's degree at Yale in the late 1990s. She was employed by them to support NASA's Mars exploration research efforts in Houston, Texas, at the Johnson Space Center. This is where she started working on the design for TransHab.

Adams came up with an inflatable design that folds up for launch and expands to a three-level home once in space. Big enough for six crew members, it also includes removable pieces that can be used for walls and furniture. Her design was also supposed to include a common room, gymnasium, and a shower. In order to make her design work, she had to research innovative ideas from other areas, such as engineering, industrial design, and sociology. Unfortunately, this project never made it past the design phase.

Even though the TransHab never came to be, Constance isn't giving up. "Someday I'd like to apply these principles to terrestrial projects," she says. "We need to understand how our planet and all the little systems inside of it can coexist without causing too much strain. I'd like to find a way to bring it all back home again."

D. COMPARE On a separate piece of paper, draw the Venn diagram and complete it with the similarities and differences in housing.

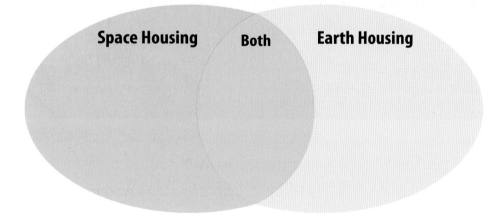

Space Housing   **Both**   **Earth Housing**

Enduring Voices

There are over 90,000 Huli speakers in Papua New Guinea, but the language is in danger of extinction because of the dependency on English.

Nowadays people learn a different language so that they can have greater opportunities in life; however, this can have a negative impact on small cultures because fewer people are using native languages. This means that the languages are in danger of becoming extinct. But there is hope: The Enduring Voices Project.

Before You Watch

WORD FOCUS

An *extinct language* is one that doesn't have any speakers.

A *dead language* is a one that is only used in special situations, but is not spoken every day.

A. Interview five classmates. Ask where they are from and what language(s) they speak.

B. Read the words and definitions. Then, complete each sentence by choosing the correct word.

disappearing	going away; dying	**enduring**	lasting forever
extinct	dead and gone	**elders**	older people
endangered	not safe or protected		

1. Many languages are _____. In fifty years, half of the languages in the world will be gone.

   a. elders   b. enduring   c. disappearing

2. Only the _____ speak the native language. The young people all speak Spanish.

   a. elders   b. enduring   c. endangered

3. The Klallam language is _____. The last known speaker died in 2014.

   a. enduring   b. disappearing   c. extinct

4. The Huli language is _____ because fewer people are speaking it.

   a. endangered   b. extinct   c. elders

5. Korean is a(n) _____ language. It is 2,600 years old and has over 65 million speakers.

   a. extinct   b. enduring   c. disappearing

C. The video you are going to watch is about disappearing languages. How do you think a language can disappear? Discuss as a class.

D. Look at the list of languages. Circle one language that you think is *dead* and discuss as a class.

English	French	Russian	Latin
Spanish	Italian	Portuguese	Korean
Mandarin Chinese	Arabic	Japanese	Vietnamese

While You Watch

A. Watch the video. Which countries do the researchers visit to study disappearing languages? Circle the correct answers.

Bhutan	Italy	Spain
United States	India	Korea
Australia	Myanmar	China

B. Put the events in order. Number the items from *1* to *6*.

1. _____ The team goes to India.

2. _____ The team goes to Australia.

3. _____ The woman teaches the team the word for *shoulder*.

4. _____ The man invites the team into his house.

5. _____ The equipment doesn't work.

6. _____ The man teaches the team the word for *father*.

C. Watch the video again. What equipment is included in the Special Language Technology Kit. Circle the equipment and write a paragraph about why it is used.

laptop computer	books on languages
maps	basic recording equipment
video camera	cell phone
CD	TV
radio	digital music player

_____

_____

_____

_____

_____

After You Watch

A. Complete the video summary with the words from the box.

elders	photographer	disappear	endangered	extinct	speaker

David Harrison and Greg Anderson study _____ languages. Chris Ranier is a _____. The three men created the Enduring Voices Project for the National Geographic Society. They want to protect languages. When we lose a language, we lose information about the speakers' culture. The men want people to know that more than half of the world's 7,000 known languages may _____ in the next 50 years. They interview a man in northern Australia. This man may be the last _____ of a language most people thought was _____.

After Australia, the team travels to northeastern India. People speak many different languages there. Many of them are in danger of being lost forever. They interview the _____ in a village. They record their language because many younger people do not speak it. If young people do not speak a language, it does not survive.

B. Read each sentence and choose *T* if a sentence is true and *F* if a sentence is false.

1. There are 2,000 known languages in the world.   T   F

2. Every two days, a language completely disappears.   T   F

3. In the northeast of India, there are many endangered languages.   T   F

4. A language can't survive if young people don't speak it.   T   F

C. Complete the table by writing answers to the questions. Discuss the questions in small groups.

Enduring Voices Project	
What do the researchers want to do?	*How do they do it?*

Health

A boy swims in a pool to train
for a triathlon.

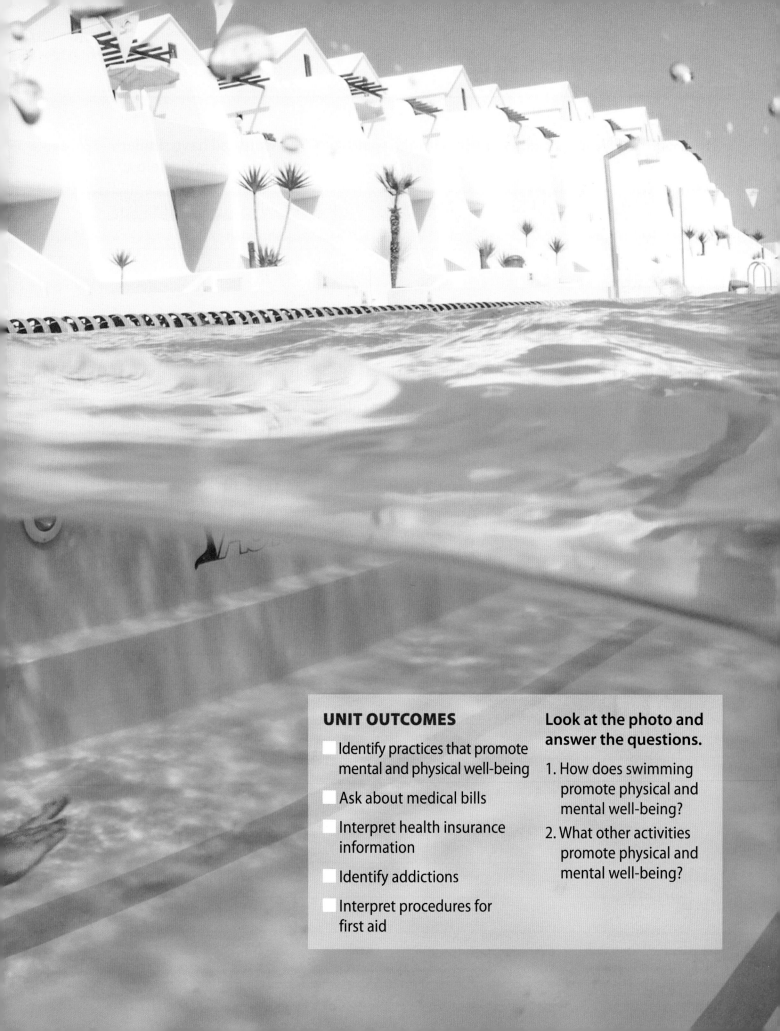

UNIT OUTCOMES

- Identify practices that promote mental and physical well-being
- Ask about medical bills
- Interpret health insurance information
- Identify addictions
- Interpret procedures for first aid

Look at the photo and answer the questions.

1. How does swimming promote physical and mental well-being?

2. What other activities promote physical and mental well-being?

Vocabulary Builder

A. A *word family* is a group of words with the same root. The words all have similar meanings but are used as different parts of speech. Look at the example below.

Noun(s)	Verb	Adjective
survival, survivor	survive	surviving

- There were no *survivors* of the car accident.
- If cancer is detected early, there is a good chance of *survival*.
- Drugs that dissolve blood clots can help people *survive* heart attacks.
- The *surviving* passengers from the plane crash tried to find help.

B. **CATEGORIZE** Put the words into the correct columns. Then, use a dictionary to find the other forms of each word family. *Note:* Not every word family has every part of speech.

~~affecting~~	withdrawal	poisoning	depressed	tolerance
impairment	addiction	meditate	insured	treat

Noun	Verb	Adjective	Adverb
affect, affection	affect	affecting, affective, affected	affectively

C. Choose one of the word families from Exercise B that has all four parts of speech. Write a sentence using each word form. Use the example sentences in Exercise A as a model.

1. _____

2. _____

3. _____

4. _____

D. **INFER** Each expression below is related to health. What do you think each one means? Write your ideas on the lines.

1. mental health: _____

2. out of shape: _____

3. self-esteem: _____

4. at risk: _____

E. Look at the following questions. Answer the ones you feel comfortable answering.

1. What are the major health care issues facing your community? Which health care issues can be categorized as mental health issues?

_____

_____

2. Do you consider yourself in good shape? Why?

_____

_____

3. Think about people who have high self-esteem. What are their traits? What are the traits of people with low self-esteem?

_____

_____

4. Do you know your family's health history? If so, what health problems have some of your family members faced?

_____

_____

LESSON ① Mind and body

GOAL ▦ Identify practices that promote mental and physical well-being

A. Discuss the following questions in a small group.

1. Do you exercise? If so, what type of exercise do you do and how often?

2. Do you eat well? On a scale of one to ten (*ten* being the healthiest), how healthy are the foods you eat?

3. How could you make your diet healthier?

4. How much water do you drink each day?

5. Do you have a lot of stress in your life? How do you relieve stress?

🎧 B. Listen to the following people talk about how they relieve stress. Take notes.

CD TR 25

Cooper

Reason for stress:

_____

How he relieves stress:

_____

_____

Stephanie

Reason for stress:

_____

How she relieves stress:

_____

_____

Fletcher and Katie

Reason for stress:

_____

How they relieve stress:

_____

_____

C. EVALUATE Do you identify with any of these people? If yes, in what ways? If not, why not?

D. **Advice columns often appear in newspapers and online. Read the problems. Do you agree with the advice?**

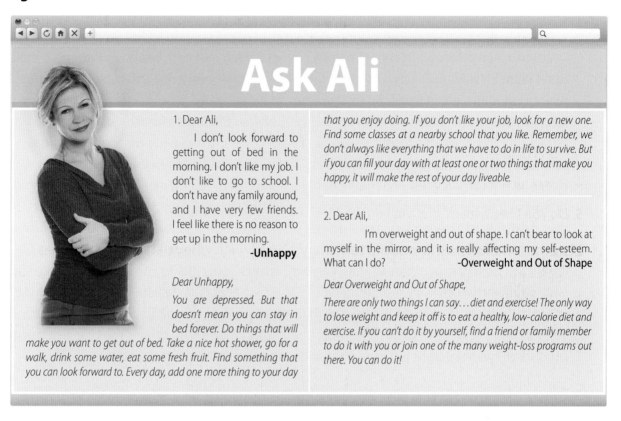

Ask Ali

1. Dear Ali,

I don't look forward to getting out of bed in the morning. I don't like my job. I don't like to go to school. I don't have any family around, and I have very few friends. I feel like there is no reason to get up in the morning.

-Unhappy

Dear Unhappy,

You are depressed. But that doesn't mean you can stay in bed forever. Do things that will make you want to get out of bed. Take a nice hot shower, go for a walk, drink some water, eat some fresh fruit. Find something that you can look forward to. Every day, add one more thing to your day that you enjoy doing. If you don't like your job, look for a new one. Find some classes at a nearby school that you like. Remember, we don't always like everything that we have to do in life to survive. But if you can fill your day with at least one or two things that make you happy, it will make the rest of your day liveable.

2. Dear Ali,

I'm overweight and out of shape. I can't bear to look at myself in the mirror, and it is really affecting my self-esteem. What can I do?   -Overweight and Out of Shape

Dear Overweight and Out of Shape,

There are only two things I can say...diet and exercise! The only way to lose weight and keep it off is to eat a healthy, low-calorie diet and exercise. If you can't do it by yourself, find a friend or family member to do it with you or join one of the many weight-loss programs out there. You can do it!

E. **SUGGEST** **Pretend you are Ali and give advice to the following people.**

Dear Ali,

My daughter is overweight. All of the kids make fun of her at school, and I think she eats even more because she is unhappy. I try to cook healthy food at home, but that doesn't seem to be helping. What can I do?—*Mother Without a Clue*

_____

_____

_____

Dear Ali,

I have a lot of stress at work. My boss pushes me pretty hard, and I want to do a good job to get ahead, but I never have any time for myself or for my family. The doctor says all the stress is giving me high blood pressure. What should I do?—*Overworked*

_____

_____

_____

F. Danielle wrote a health-related article for her school paper. Read her article.

BACK ON TRACK

I think I take pretty good care of myself. But it wasn't always that way. I used to work really long hours, eat at fast-food restaurants because they were quick and easy, and I barely ever exercised. But I got a wake-up call from the doctor one day. He said I was obese, at risk for diabetes, and that I might not make it to my fortieth birthday. From that day forward, I began to make changes in my life. I started by going for a walk every day. Now I go to the gym three times a week, walk six miles two days a week, and play volleyball with my family on the weekends. The day the doctor gave me that horrible prognosis, I went straight to the market and filled my cart with healthy food. I now make my lunch every day and cook healthy dinners for my family. My purse and my car are always filled with healthy snacks and water. If I ever get a craving for something really unhealthy, I let myself have one bite of it, and then I stick a piece of gum in my mouth. Although the exercise and eating habits really helped to lower my blood pressure and risk for diabetes, I still have quite a bit of stress in my life. To combat that, I make sure I take at least a half an hour a day for myself. Sometimes I meditate, sometimes I call a good friend, and other times I just sit down and read a book for pleasure.

G. Answer the following questions.

1. What forced Danielle to make changes in her life?

_____

2. What changes did she make?

_____

3. Do you think her article is inspiring? Why?

_____

H. CREATE With your classmates, create a health newsletter. Follow the steps below.

1. Each student writes a health article that will be inspiring to others who read it.

2. After everyone has finished his or her article, work together to edit the articles.

3. Come up with a title for your newsletter.

4. Put your newsletter together and add artwork and photos.

LESSON 2 What's this charge for?

GOAL ▌ Ask about medical bills

A. Listen to the phone conversation Linda Gregory is having with the receptionist at the doctor's office. Why is Linda confused about the amount she owes?

CD TR 26

DOCTOR		STATEMENT DATE	STATEMENT #	BALANCE DUE
Amy Rosenberg, M.D., Inc. 2880 Chestnut Ave., Ste. 340 Topeka, KS 66675 Office Phone (785) 555-0012		10/06	4689–36	$20.00

RESPONSIBLE PARTY
Mrs. Linda Gregory
56 Plains Ave.
Topeka, KS 66675

MAKE CHECK PAYABLE AND REMIT TO
AMY ROSENBERG, M.D., Inc.
2880 Chestnut Ave., Ste. 340
Topeka, KS 66675

PATIENT NAME: Gregory, Courtney			PROVIDER: Amy Rosenberg, M.D.		
DATE	**PROCEDURE**	**DESCRIPTION OF SERVICE**	**CO-PAY**	**AMOUNT PAYABLE**
8/23	99391	Well-Child Check		$100.00
8/23	90700	DTaP Vaccine		$40.00
8/23	90465	Vaccine Admin		$28.00
8/23	90645	Hib Vaccine		$32.00
8/23	90466	Vaccine Admin		$28.00
8/23		Patient Co-Pay	−$20.00	
9/01		Primary Insurance Payment		−$120.00
9/01		Uncollectible		−$68.00

B. Look at the medical bill and answer the questions.

1. Who is expected to pay this bill?

_____

2. Why did the patient go to the doctor?

_____

3. Why is the name of the responsible party different from the patient's name?

_____

4. How much is owed?

_____

5. Does anything on the bill confuse you? Write a question to ask your classmates or teacher.

_____

C. Read and listen to the following conversation between a patient and a receptionist at the doctor's office.

Receptionist:	Dr. Brook's office.
Patient:	Um, yes, this is Cooper Jackson. I came in and saw the doctor a few months ago for the pain I was having in my leg. I just received the bill, and I have a few questions.
Receptionist:	Of course, Mr. Jackson. Let me pull up your records. Do you have the date of the statement?
Patient:	Yes, it's June 16th.
Receptionist:	Ok, I have it here. How can I help you?
Patient:	Well, I don't understand what this $264 charge is for.
Receptionist:	That is for the X-rays the technician took of your leg.
Patient:	OK, but shouldn't my insurance pay for that?
Receptionist:	Yes, they might pay some. As you can see on the bill, we have billed your insurance company but are still waiting to hear back from them. Once we do, we'll send you an adjusted bill reflecting how much you owe.
Patient:	Oh, so if I don't have to pay this $264, why did you send me a bill?
Receptionist:	I know it may seem a bit confusing. Our billing department automatically sends out statements to our current patients every month, whether or not we have heard back from the insurance companies. It usually takes about a month for the bill to reflect what the insurance company has paid, so in general, if you wait two or three months to pay your bill, your statement should show the correct amount due.
Patient:	I see. That makes sense. So, I don't need to pay this bill now?
Receptionist:	No. Wait until you see an adjusted amount on there and then pay the bill.
Patient:	Great! Thanks for your help.
Receptionist:	Have a nice day, Mr. Jackson.

D. Practice the conversation with a partner. Switch roles.

E. **VISUALIZE** Practice the conversation again. This time use the information below to change the patient's questions. The receptionist will have to be creative to come up with a response.

Name	Reason for visit	Date of statement	Question
Jenna Lyn	backache	May 25th	Why isn't the payment I made showing up on the statement?
Javier Bardo	headaches	December 2nd	Do you offer discounted services? I don't have health insurance.
Kim Jensen	skin rash	March 14th	Why do I have to pay more than my co-pay?
Young Lee	ingrown toenail	July 7th	Why didn't my insurance pay for the procedure?

F. Look at the bill below and write five questions you could ask about it.

STATEMENT

Skin Care Center
5948 Atlantic Avenue
Topeka, KS 66675
Office Phone (785) 555-0198

CLOSING DATE:	7/15
BALANCE DUE:	$179.90
ACCOUNT #:	22365-1
AMOUNT ENCLOSED:	_____
PATIENT:	Linda Gregory 7653

Bill to: Linda Gregory
56 Plains Avenue
Topeka, KS 66675

Any change in the above address should be reported to our office.

Skin Care Center
5948 Atlantic Avenue
Topeka, KS 66675

DETACH AND RETURN UPPER PORTION WITH YOUR PAYMENT

Keep bottom portion for your records

PATIENT NAME: Gregory, Linda   **PROVIDER:** Elton Frank, M.D.

DATE	CODE	DESCRIPTION	CHARGE	CREDIT
2/05	99204	Office Visit New Patient	$240.00	
		Paid By Health Care PPO		$240.00
6/15	11301	Shave Skin Lesion 0.6-1.0cm	$175.00	
		Paid By Health Care PPO		$98.95
6/15	88305	Tissue Exam by Pathologist	$190.00	
		Paid By Health Care PPO		$86.15
6/15	A4550	Surgical Tray	$55.00	
		Paid By Health Care PPO		$55.00
		DUE FROM PATIENT	**$179.90**	

1. _____
2. _____
3. _____
4. _____
5. _____

G. Go over the bill with your teacher to make sure you understand everything on it.

H. Find a partner (receptionist) and have a conversation, asking him or her the questions you wrote in Exercise F. Switch roles.

LESSON ③ Health insurance

GOAL ▪ Interpret health insurance information

A. How much do you know about health insurance? In a small group, try to answer the following questions. If you need help, talk to other groups.

1. Is it mandatory in your state to have health insurance?

2. What happens if you see a doctor or go to a hospital without health insurance?

3. What is the difference between an HMO and a PPO?

B. ANALYZE Look at the chart about insured and uninsured people and answer the questions.

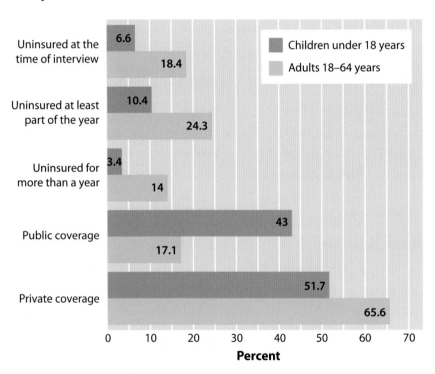

1. What is the percentage of insured adults? _____

2. What is the percentage of children who were uninsured for more than a year? _____

3. What is the percentage of adults who have private insurance? _____

4. What is the percentage of children who have public coverage? _____

C. Ask your partner questions about the information presented in the chart in Exercise B. Use the questions from the same exercise as examples.

D. Look at the chart about people without health insurance and complete the sentences below.

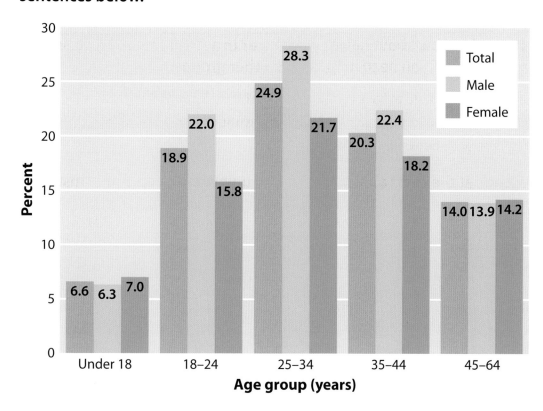

1. Of both sexes, the _____ are the most uninsured.

2. Out of all the age groups, the _____ -year-olds are the most uninsured.

3. _____ of children are uninsured.

4. _____ of children are insured.

5. _____ of women aged 35–44 are uninsured.

6. _____ of people in my age group are uninsured.

E. **ANALYZE** Write three more sentences about the statistics in the chart in Exercise D.

1. _____

2. _____

3. _____

F. Read the chart about insurance coverage and demographics. Then, write six questions based on the data.

Selected characteristic	Uninsured at the time of interview	Public health plan coverage	Private health insurance coverage
	Percent (standard error)		
Race/Ethnicity			
Hispanic or Latino	34.5 (1.14)	20.2 (0.87)	46.0 (1.25)
Non-Hispanic:			
White, single race	12.3 (0.39)	14.5 (0.46)	74.6 (0.60)
Black, single race	18.0 (0.83)	30.4 (0.99)	53.0 (1.18)
Asian, single race	13.7 (0.87)	13.6 (1.31)	73.4 (1.61)
Other races and multiple races	21.1 (2.36)	23.8 (2.13)	56.7 (2.95)
Education			
Less than high school	34.0 (1.23)	34.6 (1.22)	32.4 (1.22)
High school diploma or GED[4]	23.2 (0.65)	21.8 (0.66)	56.4 (0.80)
More than high school	10.6 (0.38)	12.2 (0.38)	78.5 (0.54)
Employment status			
Employed	15.3 (0.42)	9.4 (0.31)	75.9 (0.50)
Unemployed	43.1 (1.38)	28.5 (1.48)	28.6 (1.39)
Not in workforce	15.9 (0.69)	41.0 (0.89)	46.8 (.096)

1. _____

2. _____

3. _____

4. _____

5. _____

6. _____

G. Ask three classmates the questions you wrote in Exercise F.

H. **CREATE** In a small group, choose one of the three graphs or charts presented in this lesson. Recreate the data using information from the students in your class.

LESSON **4** Addictions

A. Look up the word *addiction* in a dictionary. Write the definition and an example sentence that uses the word.

addiction *n.* _____

_____

_____

B. Work with a partner and brainstorm a list of addictions.

C. **FIND OUT** Match the words below to their correct definitions and write the complete sentences on a separate piece of paper. Use a dictionary if you need to.

1. Tolerance is _____.

2. Impairment is _____.

3. Substance addiction is _____.

4. Physiological dependence is _____.

5. A twelve-step program is _____.

6. Psychological dependence is _____.

7. Process addiction is _____.

8. Detoxification is _____.

9. Withdrawal is _____.

10. An addict is _____.

a. the process of giving up a substance or activity to which a person has become addicted

b. a condition in which a person is dependent on some chemical substance

c. a plan for overcoming an addiction by going through twelve stages of personal development

d. a condition in which a person requires certain activities or the intake of some substance in order to maintain mental stability

e. a condition in which a person is dependent on some type of behavior

f. an inability to carry on normal, everyday functions because of an addiction

g. the ability of the body to endure a certain amount of a substance

h. the process of adjusting to the absence of some substance or activity that a person has become addicted to

i. a person physically or emotionally dependent on a substance or an activity

j. a condition in which a person's body requires certain behaviors or the intake of some substance, without which it will become physically ill

D. Look at the list of addictions below. Which ones are substance (*S*) addictions and which ones are process (*P*) addictions? Circle your answers.

Addictions		
alcohol S P	food S P	shopping S P
caffeine S P	gambling S P	video games S P
prescription medicine S P	surfing the Internet S P	work S P
illegal drugs S P	smoking (nicotine) S P	

E. In a small group, discuss the following questions.

1. Why do people become addicts?

2. What can you do if you are addicted to something?

3. What can you do to help a friend or family member who is addicted to something?

F. **ANALYZE** Read the statements below. Do you think each person has an addiction? Circle *yes* or *no* and give a reason for each answer.

1. Although my uncle Gerry sold his car to spend more time at casinos in Las Vegas, he says he doesn't have a gambling problem.
   Addiction: yes no **Reason:** _____

2. Even though her sister spends thousands of dollars a month on her credit cards, she doesn't think she is a shopaholic.
   Addiction: yes no **Reason:** _____

3. Danielle is convinced she isn't addicted to caffeine although she has to drink two cups of coffee before she can get out of bed in the morning.
   Addiction: yes no **Reason:** _____

4. In spite of the fact that Fletcher plays video games for three hours a night instead of doing his homework, he denies he has a problem.
   Addiction: yes no **Reason:** _____

Smartphone addiction can be dangerous.

G. Study the chart with your classmates and teacher.

Adverb Clauses of Concession	
Dependent clause	**Independent clause**
Although he spends a lot of time in Las Vegas,	he says he doesn't have a gambling problem.
Even though her sister spends thousands of dollars a month,	she doesn't think she is a shopaholic.
Though she has to drink two cups of coffee before she can get out of bed in the morning,	she is convinced she isn't addicted to caffeine.
In spite of the fact that he plays video games for three hours a night,	he denies he has a problem.

Explanation: Adverb clauses of concession show a contrast in ideas. The main or independent clauses show the unexpected outcome. The unexpected outcome in the third example is that it is surprising that she thinks she isn't addicted to caffeine.

Note: The clauses can be reversed and have the same meaning. Do not use a comma if the independent clause comes first in the sentence.

Example: *She doesn't think she is a shopaholic even though she spends thousands of dollars a month.*

H. Create sentences with dependent and independent clauses. Use the ideas below and the sentences in the chart in Exercise G as examples.

Internet addiction/spends five hours a day online
shopping addiction/goes to the mall at least once a day
food addiction/weighs over 300 pounds
drug addiction/sold all his clothes to buy more drugs

1. _____

_____

2. _____

_____

3. _____

_____

4. _____

_____

I. **VISUALIZE** Imagine a good friend of yours has an addiction to something. Write about his or her addiction. How is it affecting your friend's life? How is it affecting your life? How is your friendship different because of it?

LESSON **5** **First aid**

GOAL   Interpret procedures for first aid

A. **What does a first-aid kit have in it? Use the words in the box to label each item. Write the number.**

1. adhesive bandages	2. adhesive cloth tape	3. antibiotic ointment
4. antiseptic wipes	5. aspirin	6. cold compress/ice pack
7. compress dressing	8. first-aid manual	9. hydrocortisone ointment
10. roller bandage	11. scissors	12. sterile gauze pads
13. sterile gloves	14. thermometer	15. tweezers

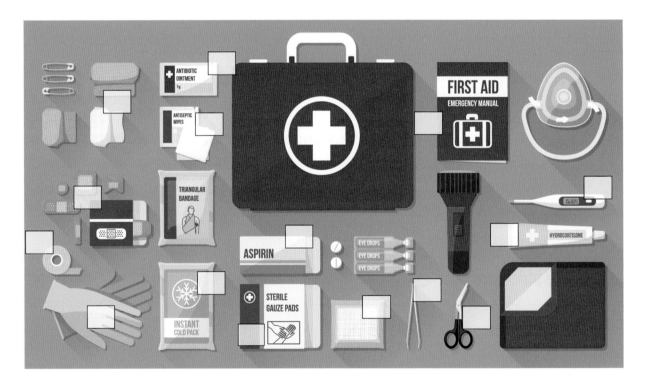

B. **Do you have a first-aid kit? Why is each item important? Discuss your ideas with your classmates.**

136   Unit 5

C. Define the following injuries.

1. burn: _____

2. choking: _____

3. poisoning: _____

4. open wound: _____

5. head injury: _____

6. shock: _____

D. APPLY Look at the list of first-aid procedures. Write the appropriate injuries on the line below each procedure.

1. Call 911.

    choking, poisoning, head injury, shock
    _____

2. Call Poison Control.

    _____

3. Control external bleeding.

    _____

4. Cover with a light gauze dressing.

    _____

5. Have the person lie down.

    _____

6. Help maintain body temperature.

    _____

7. Perform Heimlich maneuver.

    _____

8. Stop the bleeding with a piece of sterile gauze.

    _____

9. Strike the victim's back between the shoulder blades five times.

    _____

10. Treat wounds.

    _____

E. Read the information. Compare it with your answers in Exercise D. Were you right? Make a note of any difficult vocabulary and discuss as a class.

First-Aid Procedures*		
Injury	**Do**	**Don't**
burn	Run cold water over burn area for 15 minutes. Cover the burn with a light gauze dressing. If blisters pop, apply a light antibiotic ointment and cover with light gauze dressing.	**Don't** put any creams or greases on the burned area. **Don't** pop any blisters. **Don't** use an ice pack.
choking	Call 911. Strike the victim's back between the shoulder blades five times. Perform Heimlich maneuver.	**Don't** give water to the person.
poisoning	Call 911 (if person is unconscious or having trouble breathing). Call Poison Control (800-222-1222).	**Don't** induce vomiting. **Don't** give the person anything to eat or drink.
open wound	Stop the bleeding with a piece of sterile gauze. Wash with soap and water (if minor), apply a thin layer of antibiotic ointment, and cover with a bandage.	**Don't** remove any object protruding from injury. **Don't** wash or apply ointment to a large, deep wound.
head injury	Call 911 if person is unconscious or drowsy. Treat wounds. Ice a small bump.	**Don't** leave the person alone, especially when sleeping. Instead, wake up every two to three hours and have the person answer simple questions.
shock	Call 911. Have the person lie down. Control external bleeding. Help maintain body temperature.	**Don't** raise the person's head. **Don't** give the person food or drink.

* Not all first-aid procedures for each injury are listed.

F. **APPLY** Divide the class into victims and good citizens. All "victims" should write an injury from Exercise D on a piece of paper and show it to a "good citizen." Good citizens should offer advice.

EXAMPLE:

Victim: (Shows Good Citizen card that reads "Choking.")

Good Citizen says to Victim: "I'm going to call 911. Then, I'm going to strike your back five times between your shoulder blades. If that doesn't work, I'm going to perform the Heimlich maneuver. I will not give you water."

LIFESKILLS ▶ I think I might have a problem

Before You Watch

A. Look at the picture and answer the questions.

1. What is on the chair next to Naomi?

2. What problem does Hector think Naomi has?

While You Watch

B. ▶ Watch the video and complete the dialog.

Hector: Can I tell you something? I used to have an (1) _addiction_, too.

Naomi: You? (2) _____?

Hector: Yes, believe it or not. I used to be addicted to junk food. I ate it (3) _____, even when I wasn't hungry. At one point, I weighed over 250 pounds.

Naomi: You mean—you had an eating (4) _____?

Hector: You (5) _____ say that.

Naomi: What did you do about it?

Hector: Well, I (6) _____ help. I went to a counselor, and I joined a support group. I kept track of my eating, and I started working out at the gym. Pretty soon, I was addicted to going to the gym! Now, I feel a lot better.

Check Your Understanding

C. Circle the correct word in the parentheses to complete each sentence.

1. People who buy more things than they can afford are (careful shoppers /(shopaholics)).

2. When people do things they don't want to do, they may have an (addiction / addition).

3. Drug addicts and alcoholics are (depending / dependent) on substances.

4. In (support / supporting) groups, people share their experiences.

5. A (counselor / council worker) can also offer help and support.

Review

Learner Log
I can identify practices that promote mental and physical well-being.   I can ask about medical bills.
■Yes   ■No   ■Maybe   ■Yes   ■No   ■Maybe

A. Write one healthy solution for each problem.

1. Problem: I eat fast food three times a week because I have no time to cook.

   Solution: _____

2. Problem: I have high blood pressure, and I am at risk for diabetes.

   Solution: _____

3. Problem: I am really stressed at work.

   Solution: _____

4. Problem: My children are overweight.

   Solution: _____

B. Read the bill and write four questions you would ask about it.

PATIENT NAME: Reed, Jacob			PROVIDER NAME: Robert Wickern, M.D.	
DATE	**PROCEDURE**	**DESCRIPTION OF SERVICE**	**CO-PAY**	**AMOUNT PAYABLE**
8/23	99391	Well-Child Check		$150.00
8/23	90700	DTaP Vaccine		$30.00
8/23	90465	Vaccine Admin		$44.00
8/23	90645	Hib Vaccine		$32.00
8/23	90466	Vaccine Admin		$64.00
8/23		Patient Co-Pay	−$25.00	
9/17		Primary Insurance Payment		−$200.00
9/17		Uncollectible		−$75.00
			AMOUNT DUE	

1. _____

2. _____

3. _____

4. _____

C. Work with a partner and have a conversation between a patient and a person at the doctor's office with the questions you wrote. Switch roles.

Learner Log

I can interpret health insurance information. ☐ Yes ☐ No ☐ Maybe   I can identify addictions. ☐ Yes ☐ No ☐ Maybe   I can interpret procedures for first aid. ☐ Yes ☐ No ☐ Maybe

D. **Read the bar graph about health insurance coverage and answer the questions.**

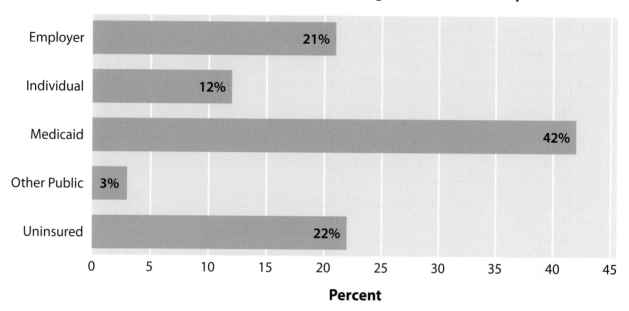

Percent

1. What is the percentage of adults who are uninsured? _____

2. What is the percentage of adults who are insured by their employers? _____

3. What is the percentage of adults who are on Medicaid? _____

4. What is the percentage of adults who have insurance coverage? _____

E. **On a separate piece of paper, write sentences combining the ideas below.**

EXAMPLE: nicotine addiction/smokes two packs of cigarettes a day

Even though he smokes two packs of cigarettes a day, he doesn't think he is addicted to nicotine.

1. exercise addiction/works out 3 times a day   2. sleeping addiction/sleeps 11 hours a night

3. food addiction/eats all day long   4. coffee addiction/drinks 4 cups a day

F. **Write down six injuries you learned about in this unit. In a group, discuss the first-aid procedures for each one.**

_____   _____   _____

_____   _____   _____

Vocabulary Review

A. Choose the correct word for each sentence.

1. _____ helps me relax when I've had a long day at work.

   a. Detoxification   b. Meditation   c. Tolerance   d. Depression

2. They think she has a sleeping pill _____.

   a. process   b. insurance   c. depression   d. addiction

3. If you are with someone who is in _____, you should call 911.

   a. shock   b. out of shape   c. meditation   d. treatment

4. How would you _____ someone who has a head injury?

   a. affect   b. treat   c. impair   d. insure

5. Jared's body has built up a _____ to alcohol since he has been drinking for so long.

   a. tolerance   b. substance   c. detoxification   d. withdrawal

B. Give two examples of each of the following items.

1. Substance addictions: _____ _____

2. Process addictions: _____ _____

3. First-aid kit items: _____ _____

4. Items on a medical bill: _____ _____

C. Write sentences using each of the following terms.

1. uninsured: _____

2. at risk: _____

3. self-esteem: _____

4. responsible party: _____

5. survive: _____

Presentation Topics

- Healthy Practices
- Medical Bills
- Health Insurance
- Addictions
- First Aid

1. **COLLABORATE** Form a team with four or five students. Decide which topic your team will work on. (Each team should choose a different topic.)

2. Choose positions for each member of your team.

Position	Job description	Student name
Student 1: Project Leader	Check that everyone speaks English. Check that everyone participates.	
Student 2: Secretary	Take notes on your team's ideas.	
Student 3: Coordinator	Divide presentation into parts. Assign each team member one part of presentation.	
Student 4: Director	Organize presentation so that individual parts create a unified whole.	
Student 5: Member	Do assigned part of presentation. Supportively critique other members' work as they rehearse their parts of presentation.	

3. Gather information for your presentation from this unit and other sources.

4. Decide how to present your material creatively. For example, you can use charts, role plays, or encourage class participation.

5. Create any materials needed for your presentation.

6. Practice your presentation.

7. Give your presentation to the class.

Disappearing Knowledge

"If they [people] knew the plants they cut down could help their children recover from illness, they might reconsider.
—Grace Gobbo

A. **PREDICT** Plants are a very important part of Grace Gobbo's work. In a group, discuss the different uses of plants.

B. Natural remedies are non-manufactured medicines that can cure illnesses. Make a list of natural remedies that you know of.

Remedy	Illness it cures

C. Read about Grace Gobbo, ethnobotanist.

For many people in Tanzania, imported pharmaceuticals are too expensive. Until recent times, it hasn't been a problem because the east African country has had traditional healers who use locally grown medicinal plants to help treat sick people. Unfortunately, this indigenous medical knowledge is disappearing and so are the plants. Grace Gobbo hopes to change that.

Grace's father was a doctor; therefore, she didn't believe in traditional healing. But once she began studying botany, she learned about plants that had successfully treated coughs and stopped bacterial infections. The evidence was too strong to ignore. Wanting to know more, Grace started interviewing traditional healers who had endless accounts of plants being used to treat skin and chest infections, diabetes, stomach ulcers, heart disease, and even mental illnesses. "Before now, these facts existed only as an oral tradition," she explains. "Nothing was written down. The knowledge is literally dying out with the elders since today's young generation considers natural remedies old-fashioned." Grace hopes that by creating a record of these natural remedies, she can convince other young people of the importance of these plants for use in curing ailments.

In addition to the traditional healers' knowledge dying with them, there is another problem: Medicinal plants are disappearing due to farming, mining, and other development. Plant products are used for fuel by most of the people in Tanzania, and agriculture is a major part of their economy. But Grace still believes people will ultimately do what is right. "I believe in people. I think if they learn and understand the value of the environment, they will make better choices. If they knew the plants they cut down could help their children recover from illness, they might reconsider. Loggers might give healers a chance to collect tree bark at the same time wood is harvested. We're working hard to bring information about sustainable agriculture and forest management to the public, and show them how to apply it."

D. SUMMARIZE On a separate piece of paper, complete each sentence with what you learned from the reading.

1. The people of Tanzania don't use imported pharmaceuticals because _____.

2. Grace wanted to learn more about traditional healing, so she _____.

3. Secrets of traditional healers are dying with them because _____.

4. Medical plants in Tanzania are disappearing because _____.

5. Grace believes that people will make better choices if they _____.

Retail

Robots in a warehouse collect orders for an online store.

UNIT OUTCOMES

- Do product research
- Purchase goods and services by phone and online
- Interpret product guarantees and warranties
- Return a product
- Sell a product

Look at the photo and answer the questions.

1. What products do you think the robots are collecting?
2. Which online store do you think owns this warehouse?

Vocabulary Builder

A. Using the words and phrases in the box, discuss the picture with a partner. Look up any words or phrases you do not know in a dictionary.

EXAMPLE: *The woman is asking the salesperson about the product warranty.*

convince	exchange	free of charge	guarantee
make	model	policy	quality
receipt	refund	research	return
review	transaction	warranty	

B. **CLASSIFY** Look at the unit outcomes. Then, look back at the words and phrases from Exercise A. Decide which words and phrases go with each outcome. (Some words and phrases can be used with more than one outcome.)

1. Do product research: _____

2. Purchase goods and services by phone and online: _____

3. Interpret product guarantees and warranties: _____

4. Return a product: _____

5. Sell a product: _____

C. Knowing a synonym for an unfamiliar word will often help you better understand its meaning. Find synonyms for the words below in a dictionary or thesaurus.

Word	Synonym
allege	
conform	
convince	
exchange	
fault	
guarantee	
malfunction	
model	
quality	
refund	
research	
return	
review	

Window shopping is one way of doing product research.

LESSON ① How much is it?

A. DETERMINE Imagine that you are going to buy the following products. In a group, discuss what information you need to research before you make your purchases. Write your ideas on the lines next to each item.

1. a bed: _____

2. a refrigerator: _____

3. a television: _____

4. a cell phone/smartphone: _____

5. an air conditioner: _____

6. a car: _____

B. Listen to the conversation Maya is having with the salesperson. What does she want to know about the patio set? Write her questions below.

CD TR 28

1. _____

2. _____

3. _____

4. _____

5. _____

6. _____

7. _____

8. _____

C. How did the salesperson answer the questions in Exercise B? Discuss the answers with your classmates.

D. Look at the list of ways to research a product. Which methods have you used before?

- Ask friends and family
- Ask a salesperson
- Go online and read product reviews
- Read a consumer magazine

E. Maya went online to research the patio furniture she saw in the store. Read the product reviews she found.

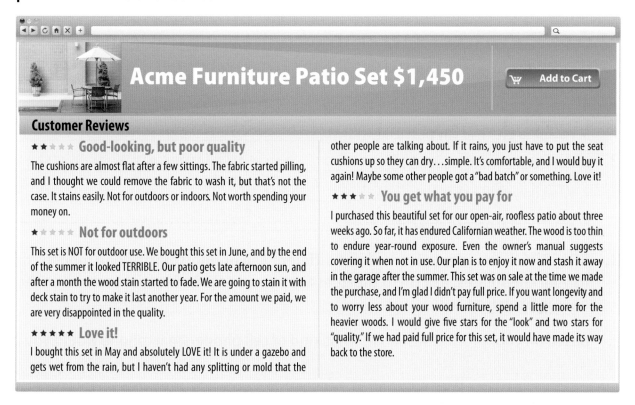

Acme Furniture Patio Set $1,450   🛒 **Add to Cart**

Customer Reviews

★★☆☆☆ **Good-looking, but poor quality**

The cushions are almost flat after a few sittings. The fabric started pilling, and I thought we could remove the fabric to wash it, but that's not the case. It stains easily. Not for outdoors or indoors. Not worth spending your money on.

★☆☆☆☆ **Not for outdoors**

This set is NOT for outdoor use. We bought this set in June, and by the end of the summer it looked TERRIBLE. Our patio gets late afternoon sun, and after a month the wood stain started to fade. We are going to stain it with deck stain to try to make it last another year. For the amount we paid, we are very disappointed in the quality.

★★★★★ **Love it!**

I bought this set in May and absolutely LOVE it! It is under a gazebo and gets wet from the rain, but I haven't had any splitting or mold that the other people are talking about. If it rains, you just have to put the seat cushions up so they can dry…simple. It's comfortable, and I would buy it again! Maybe some other people got a "bad batch" or something. Love it!

★★★☆☆ **You get what you pay for**

I purchased this beautiful set for our open-air, roofless patio about three weeks ago. So far, it has endured Californian weather. The wood is too thin to endure year-round exposure. Even the owner's manual suggests covering it when not in use. Our plan is to enjoy it now and stash it away in the garage after the summer. This set was on sale at the time we made the purchase, and I'm glad I didn't pay full price. If you want longevity and to worry less about your wood furniture, spend a little more for the heavier woods. I would give five stars for the "look" and two stars for "quality." If we had paid full price for this set, it would have made its way back to the store.

F. Based on the reviews in Exercise E, would you buy the patio furniture if it were on sale? Why?

_____

_____

G. Which review has the biggest impression on you? Why?

_____

_____

H. **EVALUATE** Think of something you have bought recently. Write a review for it on a separate piece of paper.

I. Imagine that you are buying a new cell phone/smartphone. What questions would you ask before you made your decision to purchase a particular model?

1. _____

2. _____

3. _____

J. Think about your current cell phone/smartphone. Answer the following questions.

1. What is the make and model? _____

2. How much did it cost? _____

3. Where did you buy it? _____

4. How is the quality? _____

5. Have you ever had any problems with it? _____

6. Did it come with a warranty? _____

7. What do you like about it? _____

8. What do you not like about it? _____

K. **RESEARCH** In order to learn about different cell phone/smartphone models, talk to your classmates. Ask them the questions you wrote in Exercise I as well as the ones in Exercise J.

L. Based on your product research, what kind of cell phone/smartphone would you buy?

_____

M. **RESEARCH** Choose one of the items from Exercise A to purchase. Do product research by reading reviews on the Internet or talking to your classmates. What did you find out about this product? Write some of the things you learned below.

_____

_____

_____

_____

_____

GOAL ▪ Purchase goods and services by phone and online

A. Take a class poll. How many of your classmates shop online? How many of your classmates order from catalogs by phone?

B. Look at the page from a housewares catalog. Underline each of the following pieces of information for each product: item name, item description, item price, and item number.

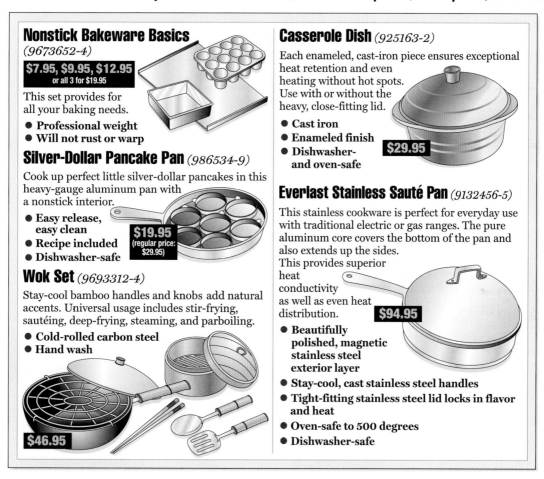

Nonstick Bakeware Basics *(9673652-4)*

$7.95, $9.95, $12.95 or all 3 for $19.95

This set provides for all your baking needs.
● Professional weight
● Will not rust or warp

Silver-Dollar Pancake Pan *(986534-9)*

Cook up perfect little silver-dollar pancakes in this heavy-gauge aluminum pan with a nonstick interior.
● Easy release, easy clean
● Recipe included
● Dishwasher-safe

$19.95 (regular price: $29.95)

Wok Set *(9693312-4)*

Stay-cool bamboo handles and knobs add natural accents. Universal usage includes stir-frying, sautéing, deep-frying, steaming, and parboiling.
● Cold-rolled carbon steel
● Hand wash

$46.95

Casserole Dish *(925163-2)*

Each enameled, cast-iron piece ensures exceptional heat retention and even heating without hot spots. Use with or without the heavy, close-fitting lid.
● Cast iron
● Enameled finish
● Dishwasher- and oven-safe

$29.95

Everlast Stainless Sauté Pan *(9132456-5)*

This stainless cookware is perfect for everyday use with traditional electric or gas ranges. The pure aluminum core covers the bottom of the pan and also extends up the sides. This provides superior heat conductivity as well as even heat distribution.
● Beautifully polished, magnetic stainless steel exterior layer
● Stay-cool, cast stainless steel handles
● Tight-fitting stainless steel lid locks in flavor and heat
● Oven-safe to 500 degrees
● Dishwasher-safe

$94.95

C. Listen to four telephone conversations between salespeople and customers who are buying items from the catalog page. Complete the table based on what you hear.

CD TR 29

	Item	Total cost	Method of payment
1.			
2.			
3.			
4.			

D. With your teacher, review the process of making a purchase online. Look for each step in the screen shots below.

1. Find the website you want to buy something from.

2. Perform a search.

3. Look at the results of your search.

4. Narrow down the results to one item.

5. Make purchase.

E. EVALUATE In a group, discuss the pros and cons of buying something online. Make two lists on a separate piece of paper.

F. What goods or services do you like to buy online? _____

_____

G. With a partner, create a list of specific items to sell in a catalog or online.

　　1. Decide what type of items you could sell.

　　2. On a separate piece of paper, create art, descriptions, and prices for at least five items.

H. Exchange your page with another pair of students. Have a conversation about purchasing the new items with your partner. One of you should be a sales representative explaining your products. Sit back-to-back to simulate selling and purchasing on the phone.

I. Do an Internet search to find items similar to the ones on the catalog page in Exercise B. Follow the steps in Exercise D to find the items you want. If you don't have computer access, answer the following questions.

　　1. What would you like to buy online? _____

　　2. What words will you type in to search for the item? _____

　　3. Do you know of an online store that sells the item? _____

　　4. Once you click on the store that sells your item, what information will you look for?

　　_____

　　5. How will you decide if you are going to purchase the item? What information will you consider?

　　_____

Be careful which websites you trust with your card details.

LESSON ❸ Is this under warranty?

GOAL ▌ Interpret product guarantees and warranties

A. Discuss the following situations with a partner and make decisions.

What would you do if . . .

1. you plugged in your new DVD player and it didn't work?

2. your printer stopped working one week after you bought it?

3. the speaker on your new cell phone/smartphone didn't work?

4. you washed a new shirt according to the care instructions on the tag and it shrank?

B. A *warranty* or *guarantee* is a written promise by a company to replace or repair a product free of charge within a certain time period after purchase if it has any defects. Read the following warranty for a set of stereo speakers.

This product is guaranteed against all defects in workmanship and materials for two years following purchase. All it takes to ensure complete coverage is to register your purchase. Once you have warranty-registered your product, the nearest service center can respond quickly and directly to you.

C. Answer the following questions about the warranty.

1. Where do you take your product if something goes wrong?

_____

2. How long is the product guaranteed?

_____

3. What do you need to do to make sure you receive the warranty for the product?

_____

4. Does the warranty cover your dropping and breaking the product?

_____

D. **Warranties are often difficult to understand because they are worded with legal language.**

> Seller warrants to the original customers purchasing products from Seller that all such products, under normal use and operation, will be free from defects in materials and workmanship affecting form, fit, and function.

In other words . . .

The seller says that if I use this product under normal conditions, as it was meant to be used, there won't be any problems with it.

E. **INTERPRET With a partner, restate each sentence below in your own words.**

1. Any claims alleging failure of products to conform to the foregoing warranty may be made only by the customer who purchased the product.

_____

_____

2. The foregoing warranty only applies while the product is being used in the original machine with the original hardware and software configuration.

_____

_____

3. Seller, at its option, will repair, replace, or provide a credit or refund of either the original purchase price less a restock fee or current fair market value, whichever is less, for any product Seller deems to be defective.

_____

_____

4. The above warranties cover only defects arising under normal use and do not include malfunctions or failures from misuse, neglect, alteration, abuse, improper installation, or acts of nature.

_____

_____

5. Removal of the labeling on products will void all warranties.

_____

_____

F. **Read the guarantee from a printer company.**

OUR NO-HASSLE GUARANTEE

Our products are backed the way they are built—the best in the industry. Our no-hassle printer guarantee gives you excellent product support with no worries. Now, you can enjoy the benefit of a substitute printer if your printer fails during the first year of use.

We will send a replacement printer to you within 48 hours of your request for any printer that fails to meet the factory specifications or fails to power up upon delivery within one year of your invoice date. Upon receipt of your no-hassle replacement printer, you must return your defective printer to us. Your defective printer will be exchanged for the same make and model, or for a printer of equal value. In addition, if your printer has three separate quality issues, which are documented with our technical support team, within one year from the date of your invoice, we will permanently replace your defective printer with a new printer of equal or greater value.

1 YEAR ✓ GUARANTEE

G. **Choose the best answer.**

1. You can receive a substitute printer if your printer doesn't work during the first . . .

   a. 48 hours.   b. year.   c. week.

2. How soon will a replacement printer be sent?

   a. within 48 hours   b. within one year   c. within one week

3. When you receive your replacement printer, you must . . .

   a. return the defective printer.   b. do nothing.   c. call the company.

4. If you have three problems with your printer during the first year, the company will . . .

   a. fix your printer for free.   b. refund your money.   c. permanently replace the printer.

H. **CREATE** **With a partner, choose a product from the list below and write your own warranty or guarantee. Use the ideas from the warranties and guarantees you have read in this lesson, but use your own words.**

digital camera   bicycle   cell phone/smartphone   washing machine

GOAL ■ Return a product

A. Think of a product you have returned to the store where you bought it. What did you return and why? Discuss your experience with your classmates.

🎧 **B.** Read and listen to the conversation.

CD TR 30

Sales Associate:	Can I help you with something?
Customer:	Yes, I'd like to return these shoes. I wore them around my house on the carpet for a few days and they are still uncomfortable. The salesman who sold them to me insisted they would stretch out and soften up, but they haven't. I'd like to get my money back.
Sales Associate:	I'm afraid I can't give you your money back. These were on sale and we don't offer refunds for sale items.
Customer:	Can I exchange them?
Sales Associate:	Yes, you can exchange them for something of equal value.
Customer:	OK, I'll do that. Let me look around for a bit.
Sales Associate:	Take your time.

🎧 **C.** Listen to each question and write the correct answer.

CD TR 31

1. _____

2. _____

3. _____

4. _____

5. _____

6. _____

Most goods can usually be returned to a store within a few weeks.

Customer Service

D. Read each return policy and the statements below them. Circle *T* (true) or *F* (false).

> Thank you for shopping at Nico's. Return or exchange for merchandise within two weeks with tags attached and/or in original packaging. Original sales receipt is required for full refund. Final sale on all sale items.

1. You can exchange sale items.   T   F

2. You need an original sales receipt for a refund.   T   F

> Valid photo ID required for all returns (except for credit card purchases), exchanges, and to receive and redeem store credit. With a receipt, a full refund in the original form of payment, except payments made with checks, will be issued for new and unread books and unopened music within four days. For merchandise purchased with a check, a store credit will be issued within the first seven days. Without an original receipt, a store credit issued by mail will be offered at the lowest selling price. With a receipt, returns of new and unread books and unopened music from our website can be made for store credit. Textbooks after 14 days or without a receipt are not returnable. Used books are not returnable.

3. If you pay with a check, you can get cash back.   T   F

4. You cannot return used books.   T   F

5. If you have a receipt, you can get a refund on unopened
   music within four days.   T   F

6. If you don't have a receipt, you can exchange an item.   T   F

> All returns and exchanges must be new, unused, and have original packaging and accessories. Some items cannot be returned if opened. For our full return and exchange policy, visit the store or log onto our website. For a gift receipt, bring this receipt back to any store within 90 days. Ask about receipt look-up.

7. All opened items can be exchanged.   T   F

> We will not be undersold. Guaranteed! If you find a lower price at any of our competitors, we will meet that price.

8. This store will offer you a lower price than its competitors.   T   F

E. Look back at all the false statements. On a separate piece of paper, rewrite each statement correctly.

F. Listen to six conversations and write the corresponding conversation number. Then, write *returned* or *exchanged*.

Conversation #	Reason for returning or exchanging item	Was item returned or exchanged?
	bought the wrong package	
	already have them	
	bad reception	
	don't fit right	
	broken	
	doesn't work with computer	

G. **SUPPOSE** Write two reasons you might return each of the items listed below.

1. digital video camera

    a. _____   b. _____

2. gallon of milk

    a. _____   b. _____

3. pair of pants

    a. _____   b. _____

4. laptop computer

    a. _____   b. _____

5. sunglasses

    a. _____   b. _____

6. textbook

    a. _____   b. _____

H. **ROLE-PLAY** Pretend you are in a store, either as a clerk or as a customer.

Clerks should help each customer with his or her return. Have at least three conversations with different customers.

Customers should choose one item from Exercise G to return or exchange. Use one of the reasons you came up with. Have at least three conversations with different clerks.

GOAL ▌ Sell a product

A. If you don't go to an actual store to get product information, you might learn about different products by reading ads. Where can you find ads? Brainstorm ideas with a partner.

B. If you were going to sell some items you owned, what would they be? Make a list on a separate piece of paper.

C. **ANALYZE** Read each of the ads below and think about the following questions.

1. What is for sale?

2. How is the seller trying to convince you to buy it?

3. Would you consider buying any of the items in the ads? Why?

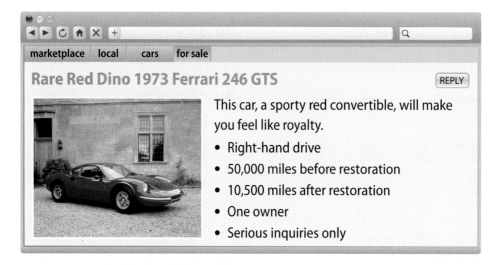

marketplace   local   cars   for sale

Rare Red Dino 1973 Ferrari 246 GTS   REPLY

This car, a sporty red convertible, will make you feel like royalty.

- Right-hand drive
- 50,000 miles before restoration
- 10,500 miles after restoration
- One owner
- Serious inquiries only

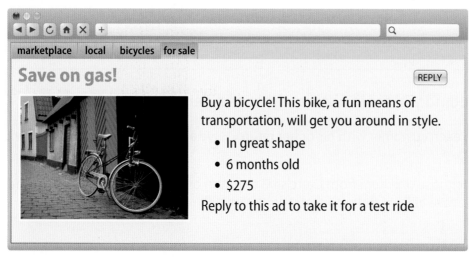

marketplace   local   bicycles   for sale

Save on gas!   REPLY

Buy a bicycle! This bike, a fun means of transportation, will get you around in style.

- In great shape
- 6 months old
- $275

Reply to this ad to take it for a test ride

D. Read about appositives with your classmates and teacher.

Appositives		
Noun or Noun Phrase	**Appositive**	**Remainder of sentence (Predicate)**
The ad,	**the one with all the great pictures,**	makes me want to buy those dishes.
That computer,	**the fastest machine in the store,**	sells for over $2,000.

Explanation:
- An appositive is a noun or noun phrase that renames another noun next to it in a sentence.
- The appositive adds extra descriptive detail, explains, or identifies something about the noun.
- An appositive can come before or after the noun phrase it is modifying.

Example: *A helpful gift, money is always appreciated by a newly married couple.*

Note: Appositives are usually set off by commas.

E. Find and underline the appositive in both ads in Exercise C.

F. Complete each of the statements below with an appositive.

1. Her dress, ____a really fancy gown____, got the attention of every customer in the room.

2. That used car, _____, will probably be for sale for quite a while.

3. Used pots and pans, _____, are hard to sell without the matching lids.

4. Two round-trip plane tickets, _____, can be used to travel anywhere in the United States.

5. The smartphone, _____, has 64 GB of storage.

6. Those leather shoes, _____, have many more years of walking in them.

7. This restaurant, _____, will make you money as soon as you open the doors.

8. That set of suitcases, _____, will carry enough clothing and accessories for two weeks of traveling.

9. Her website, _____, is an online store with tons of gently worn clothes for sale.

G. If you wanted to buy the following things, where would you look?

1. car: _____

2. shoes: _____

3. CDs (music): _____

4. furniture: _____

H. Imagine that you are going to sell something. Answer the questions below and then discuss your ideas with a partner.

1. What would you sell? _____

2. What would you say to make your product sound appealing?

_____

3. How much would you sell it for? _____

4. Where would you place your ad? _____

5. How would you want people to contact you? _____

I. Write three statements with appositives that you would use in your advertisement.

1. _____

2. _____

3. _____

J. **CREATE** On a separate piece of paper, write an ad to sell your product. Find an attractive photo to draw attention to your ad.

K. Share your ad with your classmates. See if you can find anyone who would buy what you are selling.

Smartphone apps make it easier to sell goods online.

LIFESKILLS ▶ What could go wrong?

Before You Watch

A. **Look at the picture and answer the questions.**

1. Where are Mr. and Mrs. Sanchez?

2. What are they discussing?

While You Watch

B. ▶ **Watch the video and complete the dialog.**

Mr. Sanchez: Miriam, I think you forgot to check the (1) _____sizes_____ of all these things.

Mrs. Sanchez: Victor, I think you're right. I just (2) _____ on the pictures without
(3) _____ the sizes.

Mr. Sanchez: Now, do you see why I wanted to be (4) _____?

Mrs. Sanchez: Well, I learned my lesson. (5) _____ online isn't as easy as I thought.
From now on, I will be more careful.

Check Your Understanding

C. **What are the steps in making purchases online? Write numbers to show the correct order.**

1. _____ Make your selection.

2. _____ View the products available, comparing quality and prices.

3. _____ Submit your order.

4. _____ Search for the product you want to buy.

5. _____ Log on to the merchant's website.

6. _____ Enter your payment online.

Review

A. Imagine that you are going to buy a used car. Write four questions you would ask car sellers.

1. _____

2. _____

3. _____

4. _____

B. Ask your classmates the questions you wrote in Exercise A. Write some of their responses below. When your classmates ask you their questions, you can talk about your own car or a car you are familiar with.

_____

_____

_____

C. Imagine that you are going to buy a product online. Write a short paragraph about the steps you will need to take to buy the product.

_____

_____

_____

_____

_____

D. Write a conversation between a salesperson and a customer for one of the items on page 153.

Salesperson: _____

Customer: _____

Salesperson: _____

Customer: _____

Salesperson: _____

Customer: _____

Learner Log

I can interpret product guarantees and warranties.   I can return a product.   I can sell a product.
☐ Yes ☐ No ☐ Maybe   ☐ Yes ☐ No ☐ Maybe   ☐ Yes ☐ No ☐ Maybe

E. Read the following warranty and circle *T* (true) or *F* (false).

> CLARICO warrants this product against defects in material and workmanship under normal use and service for one year from the original purchase date. CLARICO will repair or replace the defective product covered by this warranty. Please retain the dated sales receipt as evidence of the date of purchase. You will need it for any warranty service. In order to keep this warranty in effect, the product must have been handled and used as described in the instructions accompanying this warranty. This warranty does not cover any damage due to accident, misuse, abuse, or negligence.

1. This warranty is good for two years.   T   F
2. CLARICO will replace your product if it gets stolen.   T   F
3. You need your receipt to get service under this warranty.   T   F
4. This warranty covers product defects.   T   F

F. Working in pairs, use the return policy and the situations below to practice asking questions about returning items. One student is a customer and one is a clerk. Switch roles.

> Valid photo ID required for all returns (except for credit card purchases), exchanges, and to receive and redeem store credit. With a receipt, a full refund in the original form of payment, except payments made with checks, will be issued for new and unread books and unopened music within four days. For merchandise purchased with a check, a store credit will be issued within the first seven days. Without an original receipt, a store credit issued by mail will be offered at the lowest selling price. With a receipt, returns of new and unread books and unopened music from our website can be made for store credit. Textbooks after 14 days or without a receipt are not returnable. Used books are not returnable.

1. return books with the original receipt   2. return textbooks after three weeks
3. return two calendars without a receipt   4. exchange CDs that have not been opened

G. Write appositives to complete each statement below.

1. This pre-owned car, _____, has been thoroughly inspected and is in tip-top shape.

2. This laptop computer, _____, still has a two-year warranty.

3. Two theater tickets, _____, can be used any weeknight in the month of August.

4. The bicycle, _____, has barely been ridden.

H. Using one of the statements in Exercise G, write an ad for the product on a separate piece of paper. Include an appositive in the ad.

Vocabulary Review

A. **Use the following words in a sentence.**

1. allege: _____

2. guarantee: _____

3. quality: _____

4. convince: _____

5. malfunction: _____

6. policy: _____

B. **Share your sentences with a partner. Write your partner's best sentence below.**

_____

C. **Match each word to its synonym.**

Word	Synonym
1. return _____	a. claim
2. refund _____	b. promise
3. model _____	c. match
4. guarantee _____	d. replace
5. exchange _____	e. reimburse
6. convince _____	f. persuade
7. conform _____	g. type
8. allege _____	h. take back

Create an online or catalog-only store

1. **COLLABORATE** Form a team with four or five students. Choose positions for each member of your team.

Position	Job description	Student name
Student 1: Project Leader	Check that everyone speaks English. Check that everyone participates.	
Student 2: Secretary	Take notes on your team's ideas.	
Student 3: Designer	Design layout of catalog or web page.	
Student 4: Director	Assign each team member one part of presentation. Organize presentation so that individual parts create a unified whole.	
Student 5: Assistant	Help secretary and designer with their work.	

2. Decide the name of your store and what you will sell. Select a variety of items to sell.

3. Create the following items for your store: catalog or web page, the store's return policy, and a warranty/guarantee policy.

4. Prepare a poster that contains all of the information in Steps 2 and 3.

5. Present your store's catalog pages or web page to the class.

EXPLORER BRYAN CHRISTY

The Ivory Trade

"The illegal ivory trade is clearly organized crime. The surprising thing is that it's taken them so long to call it that."
—Bryan Christy

A. PREDICT Look at the small picture and answer the questions.

1. What do you see? Do you think this is a good thing or a bad thing? Why?

2. How much do you think an elephant tusk is worth?

3. Does an elephant regrow its tusk if it is removed?

B. Read about Bryan Christy and the ivory trade.

Did you know that in China, a pair of ivory chopsticks could cost more than one thousand dollars? And that a carved elephant tusk could sell for hundreds of thousands of dollars? Bryan Christy does. He is an investigative reporter who has worked for years covering the illegal ivory trade. He is also the director of special investigations for *National Geographic* magazine and was named National Geographic Explorer of the Year in 2014 for his work on international wildlife trafficking. According to Christy, "The illegal ivory trade is clearly organized crime. The surprising thing is that it's taken them so long to call it that."

The middle class in China is growing by leaps and bounds, and products made of ivory are popular. On the contrary, poverty is devastating Africa, where most of the ivory comes from. If people in Africa can sell this product, what is the problem? The problem is that in order to get the ivory from an elephant, you must kill it and remove its tusks.

Over 30,000 African elephants are killed every year. In fact, more than 100,000 were slaughtered between 2010 and 2012. How is this happening? Poor villagers and unpaid park rangers are killing these elephants for cash. Even though it's against the law, the money is worth more than the possible punishment. But it has gotten even worse. Now military and terrorist groups, who are partially funded by trading ivory, are traveling from their home countries, hiding out inside national parks, and poaching elephants, too. They're stealing from local communities, enslaving local villagers, and killing park rangers to get to the elephants. They want the ivory to sell so that they can purchase ammunition.

The only way to stop this unlawful killing of elephants is to ban the trading of ivory. In September of 2015, the presidents of the United States and China agreed to work together on banning the import and export of ivory. But the success of these bans may be limited in China because ivory is still an important commodity there.

C. Fact or Opinion? Write *F* in front of each fact and *O* in front of each opinion.

1. _____ Over 30,000 African elephants are killed every year.

2. _____ Poverty is devastating Africa.

3. _____ Bryan Christy was named National Geographic Explorer of the Year in 2014.

4. _____ A pair of chopsticks made out of ivory costs more than one thousand dollars.

5. _____ The only way to stop this unlawful killing of elephants is to ban the trading of ivory.

D. DEFEND What is your opinion on the ivory trade? Write a paragraph explaining your point of view.

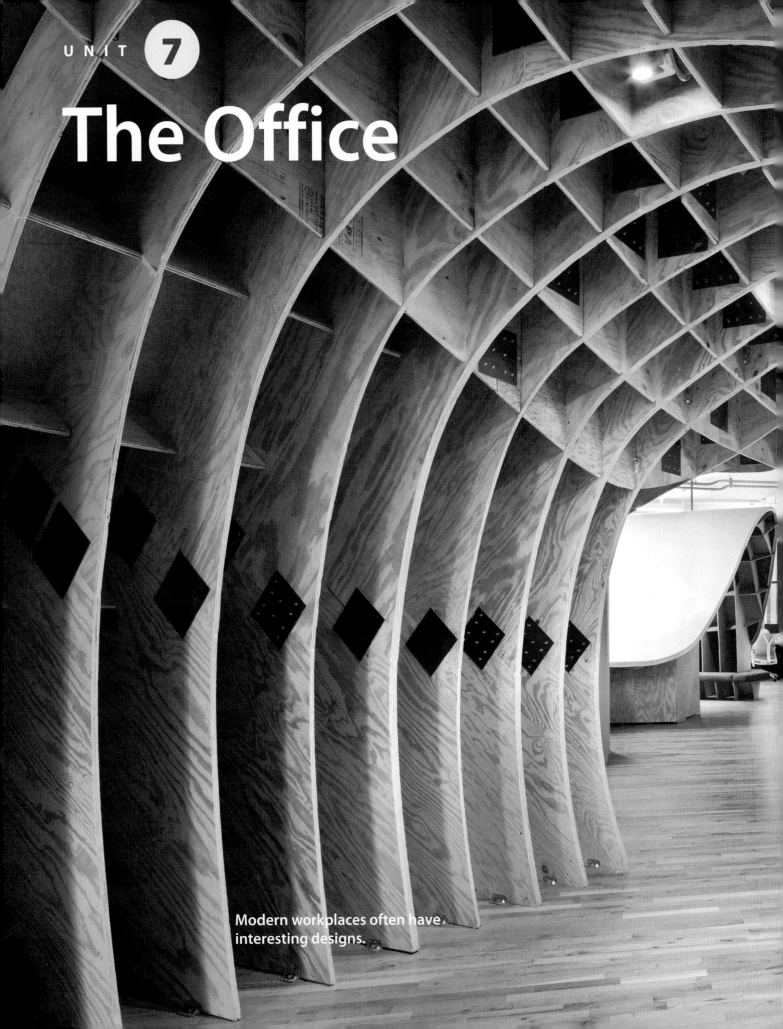

UNIT **7**

The Office

Modern workplaces often have interesting designs.

UNIT OUTCOMES

☐ Identify and use technology

☐ Resolve technology problems

☐ Establish an organizational system

☐ Identify and resolve problems at work

☐ Report progress

Look at the photo and answer the questions.

1. What technology might you find in an office like this?

2. What do you think the people at the table are discussing?

Vocabulary Builder

A. EXPLAIN Use the terms in the box below to label each item you might find in an office. Under each item, write a brief description of its purpose.

business telephone	external hard drive	LCD projector	photocopier
~~laptop computer~~	USB stick	paper shredder	printer

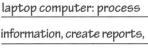

laptop computer: process
information, create reports,
and do Internet research

_____
_____
_____

_____
_____
_____

_____
_____
_____

_____
_____
_____

_____
_____
_____

_____
_____
_____

B. A great way to remember vocabulary is to draw pictures. Draw pictures for the following terms. Use a dictionary to look up any words you don't know, but remember to look for the definition that is related to technology.

headset	cable	port	memory card

C. The three following technology terms cannot be drawn easily. Write a definition for each one.

1. troubleshoot: _____

2. paper jam: _____

3. feed: _____

D. Look at the verbs in the table below. Find the nouns and adjectives in the verbs' word families.

Verb	Noun	Adjective
compete		
collaborate		
avoid		
accommodate		
compromise		
motivate		
resolve		

LESSON **1** # How do you turn it on?

GOAL ▊ Identify and use technology

A. Read the instructions for connecting a printer to a computer.

1. Take the **printer** out of the box and set it next to your **computer**.

2. Make sure the printer is **off**.

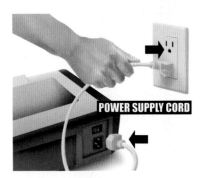

3. Plug the **power supply cord** into the back of the printer and then plug it into the wall socket.

4. Plug one end of the **USB cable** into the **USB port** on the back of the printer. Plug the other end into the **USB port** on the computer.

B. SUMMARIZE Reread the instructions in Exercise A. Then, in your own words, tell a partner how to connect a printer to a computer. (If you have a computer and printer in your classroom, you can explain the steps as you do them.)

C. Connecting a projector to a computer is similar to connecting a printer. Match the instructions below to the correct picture. Then, label each picture.

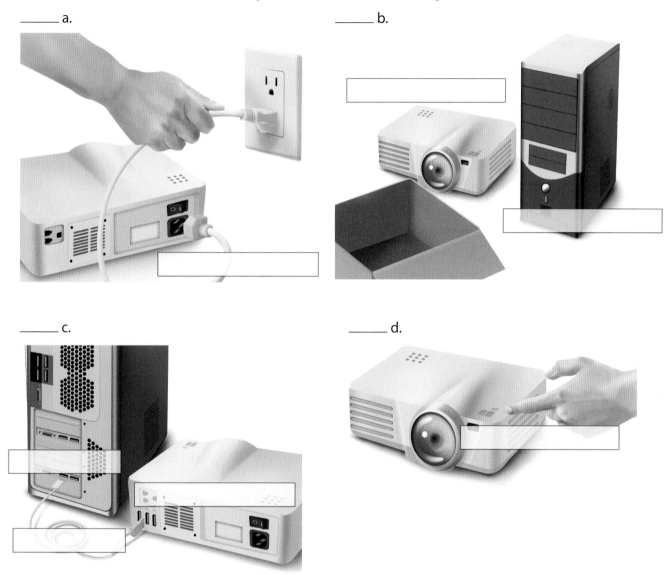

_____ a.

_____ b.

_____ c.

_____ d.

1. Take the **projector** out of the box and set it next to your **computer**.

2. Make sure the projector is **off**.

3. Plug the **power supply cord** into the back of the projector and then plug it into the wall socket.

4. Plug one end of the **firewire cable** into the **firewire port** on the back of the projector. Plug the other end into the **firewire port** on the computer.

D. **Read the excerpt from a fax machine manual and answer the questions that follow.**

How to send a fax

1 Place the document (up to 15 pages) to be sent in the document feeder.

2 Enter the fax number in one of the following ways:
- Use the dial pad.
- Select the number from the address book (see *Address Book* on page 15).
- Use the speed dial function (see *Speed Dialing* on page 16).

3 Press **Start.**

📝 Note ――――――――――――――――
To cancel, press **Stop/Exit.** ⊙

How to receive a fax

There are three modes for receiving faxes:
- Fax mode: The machine will automatically answer each call as a fax (See *Fax Mode* on page 21).
- Auto answer mode: The telephone rings for a certain number of rings and then switches to fax (See *Auto Answer Mode* on page 22).
- Manual mode: The telephone will ring. Press **Start** to receive the fax (See *Manual Mode* on page 23).

1. When sending a fax, how many different ways are there to enter a fax number? _____

2. Which method of sending a fax doesn't require pushing the start button? _____

3. How many pages can you fax at once? _____

4. How many modes are there to receive a fax? _____

5. Which mode for receiving a fax requires that you press the start button? _____

E. **GENERATE** **Look back at the list of technology items on pages 174 and 175. Choose one item that you are familiar with and write a list of instructions with illustrations. Review your instructions with a partner.**

LESSON **2** How do you fix it?

GOAL ▓ Resolve technology problems

A. Think of some problems you have had in the past with technology. In a small group, discuss what the problems were and how you fixed them.

B. Carla is having trouble with her printer. No paper comes out when she tries to receive a fax. Read what she found in her manual about *troubleshooting*.

Problem	Solution
Paper jams during printing.	Remove the jammed paper by pulling it out gently. If the paper tears while you are removing it, make sure that no small pieces are left inside the machine.
Paper sticks together.	Make sure you do not have more than 40 sheets in the paper tray. Take the paper out, fan the pages, and put them back in. Note: Humidity can cause pages to stick together.
Paper will not feed.	Remove any obstructions from inside the printer.
Multiple sheets of paper feed at the same time.	When loading the paper, do not force the paper down into the printer. If multiple sheets have caused a paper jam, clear it.

C. Answer the questions based on the troubleshooting guide in Exercise B.

1. What should you do if paper tears while you are removing it from the printer?

_____

2. How many sheets can the paper tray hold? _____

3. What causes pages to stick together? _____

4. What should you do if the paper won't feed? _____

_____

5. What should you do if there is a paper jam? _____

_____

D. **SUGGEST** Read Carla's problem in Exercise B again. What are three suggestions you might give her?

1. _____

2. _____

3. _____

E. Listen to the conversations between employees at a small printing company. Write the problems and suggestions for fixing them in the table below.

Problem	Suggestions
	1. 2.
	1.
	1. 2. 3.

F. Maya has to take pictures for her job as a home appraiser. She is having some problems with her digital camera. Match each problem to its possible solution.

1. Camera will not operate. _____

2. Camera won't take any more pictures or video. _____

3. Only a few pictures will fit on the memory card. _____

4. Battery loses its charge quickly. _____

5. Pictures won't display on the LCD screen. _____

a. Turn LCD screen on.

b. Turn camera on.

c. Replace battery.

d. Clear memory card.

e. Take pictures at a lower resolution.

G. Read the troubleshooting guide for a label maker.

Problem	Solution
1. The display stays blank after you have turned on the machine.	Check that the AC adaptor is connected correctly. If you are using batteries, check that they are inserted correctly. If the batteries are low on power, replace them.
2. The machine doesn't print or the printed characters are blurred.	Check that the tape cassette has been inserted properly. If the tape cassette is empty, replace it. Make sure the tape compartment cover has been closed.
3. The text files that you stored in the memory are no longer there.	Replace the batteries.
4. A blank horizontal line appears through the printed label.	Clean the printhead.
5. Striped tape appears.	You have reached the end of the tape. Replace the tape cassette with a new one.

H. Read the troubleshooting guide for the label maker in Exercise G again. Check (✓) the best answers.

1. You should clean the printhead when . . .

☐ a. striped tape appears.

☐ b. a horizontal line appears.

☐ c. the display is blank.

2. When your files from memory are no longer there, you should . . .

☐ a. connect the AC adaptor.

☐ b. clean the printhead.

☐ c. replace the batteries.

3. If the printed characters are blurred, you should . . .

☐ a. make sure the tape compartment cover has been closed.

☐ b. replace the batteries.

☐ c. clean the printhead.

4. What does it mean when striped tape appears?

☐ a. The printhead is dirty.

☐ b. The tape cassette needs to be replaced.

☐ c. The tape compartment needs to be closed.

I. **SUGGEST** In a small group, ask for help with the technology problems below. Write suggestions in the table.

Problem	Suggestions
My fax machine won't send a fax.	
There is no dial tone on my telephone.	
My printer won't print.	
My paper shredder won't shred.	
The copier keeps jamming.	

J. **JUDGE** Share the suggestions you received from your classmates for the problems in Exercise I. Which suggestions are the best?

GOAL ▓ Establish an organizational system

A. CLASSIFY One way of organizing things is by putting similar items in groups. How would you organize this supply closet? Discuss your solutions with your classmates.

B. On a separate piece of paper, reorganize the supply closet. Do a simple drawing of the closet and show where you would keep each item.

C. Each folder represents a place to file certain documents. Look at the list and match each document with its folder. Write the letters on the folders.

a. Bank of the East Statement for March

b. Canyon i867 User Guide

c. City National Bank Statement for April

d. Claire's Order #7654

e. Delpi Photo Plus Manual

f. Dresses 'n' More Order #7625

g. Fancy Pants Return #7986

h. HL Printer 5000 User Guide

i. Jimbo's Return #7893

j. Leapin' Lizards Return #5678

k. Pink Lady Order #6879

l. Sunshine Girls Order #9864

Purchase Orders	Bank Statements
	a

Returns	Manuals

D. One way of organizing things is by putting them in alphabetical order. Rewrite the list of folders in Exercise C in alphabetical order.

1. _____ 2. _____

3. _____ 4. _____

E. **CLASSIFY** Organize the purchase orders and returns in Exercise C in numerical order.

Purchase Orders	Returns
1. _____	1. _____
2. _____	2. _____
3. _____	3. _____
4. _____	

F. Lars needs to get organized in his home office. Read about his problem and solution.

Problem: My financial papers are very disorganized. They are in huge piles on my desk and in my desk drawers.

Solution: I'm going to buy hanging files and file folders. The tabs on my hanging files will be labeled as follows: *Bank Accounts, Credit Cards, Income, Investments, Retirement Accounts, Liabilities, Insurance, Real Estate,* and *Tax Returns.* Each hanging folder will be a different color and inside there will be file folders of that same color. For example, in my *Bank Account* file, there will be a file folder for each of the three banks where I have accounts. Inside those folders, I will keep my bank statements and any papers related to those accounts.

G. SOLVE In a small group, come up with organizing solutions for the problems below.

1. **Problem:** There are over 300 books scattered about the office—in bookcases, on people's desks, and on the floor next to desks.

   Solution: _____

   _____

2. **Problem:** The supply closet has supplies everywhere; nothing can be found.

   Solution: _____

   _____

3. **Problem:** My papers are very disorganized; there are stacks of papers everywhere.

   Solution: _____

   _____

H. Think of an organizational problem you have at home. Describe the problem below and write out a detailed solution.

_____

_____

_____

_____

_____

LESSON **4** What's the problem?

GOAL ▦ Identify and resolve problems at work

A. Answer the following questions with a partner.

1. What is *conflict resolution*?

2. Where are some places that conflicts might occur?

3. Who are some people that you might have conflicts with?

4. Think about the ways you handle conflicts with people. What would you say your personal style of behavior is when speaking to people in a conflict?

B. PREDICT Read the questions before each section of the article. Think about them as you read and answer them after you finish reading.

1. What are the three benefits of resolving conflict?

2. What can happen if conflict is not handled effectively?

Conflict Resolution: Resolving Conflict Rationally and Effectively

In many cases, conflict in the workplace just seems to be a fact of life. The good news is that by resolving conflict successfully, you can solve many of the problems that it has brought to the surface, as well as get benefits that you might not at first expect:

1. **Increased understanding:** The discussion needed to resolve conflict expands people's awareness of the situation, giving them an insight into how they can achieve their own goals without undermining those of other people.

2. **Increased group cohesion:** When conflict is resolved effectively, team members can develop stronger mutual respect and a renewed faith in their ability to work together.

3. **Improved self-knowledge:** Conflict pushes individuals to examine their goals in close detail, helping them understand the things that are most important to them, sharpening their focus, and enhancing their effectiveness.

However, if conflict is not handled effectively, the results can be damaging. Conflicting goals can quickly turn into personal dislike. Teamwork breaks down. Talent is wasted as people disengage from their work. And it's easy to end up in a vicious downward spiral of negativity and recrimination.

3. What are the five different conflict styles in Thomas and Kilmann's theory?

Understanding the Theory: *Conflict Styles*

In the 1970s, Kenneth Thomas and Ralph Kilmann identified five main styles of dealing with conflict that vary in their degrees of cooperativeness and assertiveness:

Competitive: People who tend towards a competitive style take a firm stand and know what they want. They usually operate from a position of power, drawn from things like title, rank, expertise, or persuasive ability.

Collaborative: People tending towards a collaborative style try to meet the needs of all people involved.

Compromising: People who prefer a compromising style try to find a solution that will at least partially satisfy everyone.

Accommodating: This style indicates a willingness to meet the needs of others at the expense of the person's own needs.

Avoiding: People tending towards this style seek to evade the conflict entirely.

People tending towards a collaborative style try to meet the needs of all people involved.

4. What are the five steps for resolving conflict?

Using the Tool: *A Conflict-Resolution Process*

Step One: Set the scene.

Make sure that people understand that the conflict may be a mutual problem, which may be best resolved through discussion and negotiation rather than through raw aggression.

Step Two: Gather information.

Here, you are trying to get to the underlying interests, needs, and concerns of the other people involved. Ask for the other people's viewpoints and confirm that you respect their opinions and need their cooperation to solve the problem.

Step Three: Agree on the problem.

This sounds like an obvious step, but often different underlying needs, interests, and goals can cause people to perceive problems very differently. You'll need to agree on the problems that you are trying to solve before you'll find a mutually acceptable solution.

Step Four: Brainstorm possible solutions.

If everyone is going to feel satisfied with the resolution, it will help if everyone has had fair input in generating solutions. Brainstorm possible solutions and be open to all ideas, including ones you never considered before.

Step Five: Negotiate a solution.

By this stage, the conflict may be resolved—both sides may better understand the position of the other, and a mutually satisfactory solution may be clear to all.

C. **SUMMARIZE** **Choose one of the following topics and write a one-paragraph summary.**

1. The benefits of conflict resolution

2. Thomas and Kilmann's five conflict styles

3. The five steps of the conflict-resolution process

_____

_____

_____

_____

_____

GOAL ▦ Report progress

A. Maria's supervisor has asked her to write a progress report about a long-term project she is working on. Read the guidelines he gave her.

> **Progress Report Guidelines**
>
> You write a progress report to inform a supervisor, associate, or customer about progress you've made on a project over a certain period of time. In the progress report, you explain all of the following:
>
> - what the project is
> - how much of the work is complete
> - which part of the work is currently in progress
> - what work remains to be done
> - what problems or unexpected issues have arisen

B. **ANALYZE** Read part of Maria's report. Is she following the guidelines so far?

> **To:** Henry Kim, Human Resources Director
> **From:** Maria Avalos
> **Date:** April 14th
> **Subject:** Program for Employee Training
>
> It seems that many problems have arisen from the employees working such long hours and not being able to communicate effectively with one another. It was proposed that I put together a training program for our employees on conflict resolution.
>
> So far, I have been conducting research on whether it is better to bring in an outside training organization or do the training ourselves. I have concluded that it would be more cost-effective for us to do the training ourselves. So, I am currently working on putting together a training manual that can be used for the conflict-resolution training. I foresee that it will take me another two weeks to complete the manual. Once it has been completed, we will need to choose several people to conduct the training and train them to be effective leaders.

C. Is anything missing from Maria's report? If so, include details of what is missing below.

_____

_____

D. Study the chart with your classmates and teacher.

Noun Clauses as Objects		
Subject + Verb	**Noun clause**	**Explanation**
I did	*what* I was asked.	
She knows	*how* the computer works.	• A noun clause starts with a question word or *that* and is followed by a subject and verb.
They decided	*where* the location would be.	
My boss asked	*who* would be best for the job.	• In these examples, the noun clauses are the objects of the sentences.
I hope	*that* they work as a team.	

E. Complete each of the sentences below with an appropriate noun clause from the list. More than one noun clause may be appropriate.

how the filing system worked	where the files were stored
~~what she told me to~~	who got to receive the training
that they would be promoted	how to complete the progress report
that we knew what we were doing	who wanted to be the team leader

1. I did *what she told me to* _____.

2. She found _____.

3. The supervisor asked _____.

4. He explained _____.

5. Our team showed _____.

6. Sari asked _____.

7. Jared and Giulia hoped _____.

8. The representative chose _____.

F. Complete each sentence with a noun clause of your own.

1. I asked _____.

2. I hoped _____.

3. I decided _____.

4. I explained _____.

G. SUGGEST Maria reports that she has encountered problems. Read the problems and write a paragraph from Maria's perspective. Include what she might suggest as solutions.

- The employees do not want this training.

- None of the supervisors who could be trainers want to lead the training.

_____

_____

_____

_____

_____

_____

_____

_____

H. Write a progress report using the guidelines in Exercise A. Use the format of Maria's report in Exercise B and the information below. Using the examples in Exercises D and E, include noun clauses in your report.

Project: Change the way scheduling of staff is handled.

Work completed: Servers and bartenders have been interviewed.

Doing now: Interviewing the kitchen staff.

To do: Take information from interviews and come up with a better way to handle scheduling in the future.

Problems: Last-minute shift switching without manager approval; some shifts are too short.

You seem to be doing a very good job

Before You Watch

A. Look at the picture and answer the questions.

1. Where are Hector and Mr. Patel?

2. What are they discussing?

While You Watch

B. ▶ **Watch the video and complete the dialog.**

Mr. Patel: This stick on the side is called a (1) _____. You can use it to operate the functions on the screen. There's a keypad on the bottom.

Hector: That's really cool. The (2) _____ is so clear, and it's really big.

Mr. Patel: And there are (3) _____ on both sides for things like charging the battery, inserting the flash memory card, etc. With a USB cable, you can directly download things from your computer.

Hector: That's great! This is a really useful little (4) _____.

Mr. Patel: Yes, it is. You can send e-mails from this, you can receive calls, and you can store all sorts of (5) _____.

Check Your Understanding

C. Watch the video. Read the statements and write *T* for true and *F* for false.

1. _____ Mr. Patel says that Mateo has been doing a good job.

2. _____ Hector is going to manage the women's department.

3. _____ Hector can send e-mails from his PDA.

4. _____ Hector can connect the PDA to his computer.

5. _____ Other employees can reach Hector on his PDA at any time.

6. _____ The stick on the side is a pen.

Review

Learner Log

I can identify and use technology.
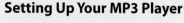
☐ Yes ☐ No ☐ Maybe

I can resolve technology problems.
☐ Yes ☐ No ☐ Maybe

A. Read the instructions for setting up an MP3 player and answer the questions that follow.

> **Setting Up Your MP3 Player**
>
> Step 1: Charge the battery.
> Step 2: Install the software.
> Step 3: Import music to your computer.
> Step 4: Connect the MP3 player to your computer and transfer music.
> Step 5: Play music.

1. What do you need to do before you import music to your computer?

   _____

2. What can you do after you have transferred music?

   _____

3. What is the first thing you must do?

   _____

4. What must you do in order to be able to transfer music?

   _____

B. Read the tips and troubleshooting advice for an MP3 player. Then, choose the best answers.

> Most problems can be resolved by resetting your MP3 player.
>> To reset your MP3 player:
>> 1. Connect it to a power outlet using the power adaptor.
>> 2. Toggle the **Hold** switch on and off.
>> 3. Press and hold the **Menu** button for at least 10 seconds.
>
> If your player won't turn on or respond:
> • Make sure the **Hold** switch is off.
> • If you're using the remote, make sure the remote's **Hold** switch is off.
> • Recharge your battery.

1. You can solve most problems with your MP3 player by . . .
   a. recharging the battery.   b. turning it on and off.   c. resetting it.

2. Which button do you hold down when resetting the player?
   a. Hold   b. Menu   c. Power Adaptor

3. What's the first thing you should do to reset your player?
   a. Make sure the *Hold* switch is off.
   b. Connect it to a power outlet.
   c. Hold down the *Menu* button.

Learner Log

I can establish an organizational system.   I can identify and resolve problems at work.   I can report progress.
■ Yes ■ No ■ Maybe   ■ Yes ■ No ■ Maybe   ■ Yes ■ No ■ Maybe

C. Alphabetize the following items on a separate piece of paper.

paper shredder	telephone	scanner
USB stick	external hard drive	projector
computer	printer	cable
fax machine	power adaptor	

D. How would you organize the items in Exercise C in an office?

_____

_____

_____

_____

E. Answer the following questions about the conflict-resolution article on pages 185–187.

1. What are the three benefits to resolving conflict?

   a. _____

   b. _____

   c. _____

2. What are the five different conflict styles in Thomas and Kilmann's theory?

   a. _____   b. _____

   c. _____   d. _____

   e. _____

3. What are the five steps for resolving conflict?

   a. _____   b. _____

   c. _____   d. _____

   e. _____

F. Write the five things a progress report should include.

   a. _____   b. _____

   c. _____   d. _____

   e. _____

Vocabulary Review

A. Put each word below in the correct column according to its part of speech: *noun, verb,* or *adjective.*

cost-effective	reorganize	organize	hanging files	fan
feed	effective	splotchy	paper jam	long-term
obstructions	force	faded	toner	power supply

Noun

1. _____

2. _____

3. _____

4. _____

5. _____

Verb

1. _____

2. _____

3. _____

4. _____

5. _____

Adjective

1. _____

2. _____

3. _____

4. _____

5. _____

B. Use words from Exercise A to complete the sentences. Not all the words are used.

1. Did you get a chance to put the _____ in alphabetical order?

2. The computer wasn't working because the _____ wasn't plugged in.

3. If you _____ out the paper, it shouldn't stick together so much.

4. It doesn't seem _____ to have so many computers running at the same time. That wastes a lot of energy.

5. Tim, can you _____ these files? They seem to have gotten out of order.

6. If you _____ the paper into the feeder, it will probably cause a

   _____ .

7. When I opened up the fax machine, I couldn't see any _____ .

8. We need a/an _____ solution to this disorganized supply closet.

9. Is there any more _____ in the supply closet? These copies are

   _____ and _____ .

10. I wonder why the paper won't _____ through the printer correctly?

RESEARCH PROJECT ✓ Looking for a job

A. In the past two units, you have learned about two different areas of work: the retail setting and the office. In a group, brainstorm a list of jobs that might be found in each of these areas.

Retail jobs	Office jobs

B. Look back at your two lists. Circle the jobs that you think earn the most money.

C. Using the Internet or printed materials from your teacher, research jobs and see if you can add to your lists in Exercise A.

D. Choose two or three jobs that seem the most interesting to you and find out the following information.

Job title	Salary	Training/Qualifications required	Related occupations

Crisis Mapping

"We're proving what can happen when ordinary people become digitally empowered, collaborate, and use technology to make a positive, lifesaving difference. It's incredibly rewarding, reassuring, and inspiring."
—Patrick Meier

A. PREDICT Read the title and the quote. What do you think the relationship between the two is?

B. Discuss the social media terms and websites with a partner. Which are you familiar with? Which do you use? Are there other websites you use that are not listed?

crowdsourcing	Facebook	texting	Instagram
e-mailing	Snapchat	tweeting	Twitter

C. Read about Patrick Meier.

Patrick Meier has come up with a way to use technology to help save lives. But not in a hospital, like you might think. He is leading the way in the field of crisis mapping. Patrick maps important information that is posted in real time from social media. The maps are full of information and available for free to humanitarian organizations and their volunteers so that they can provide help to those in need.

Patrick is the director of crisis mapping at a nonprofit technology company formed in 2008 called Ushahidi, which means *witness* in Swahili. Ushahidi provides a place for anyone to gather information and create live multimedia maps using crowdsourced information. He's also the co-founder of the Standby Task Force (SBTF). This company and task force together have changed and strengthened relief efforts around the world. Organizations such as the United Nations, U.S. Marines and Coast Guard, the World Health Organization, and Amnesty International can access these crisis maps.

So how does it work? As disaster strikes, whether it be an earthquake, a tsunami, a fire, or a hurricane, people start e-mailing, texting, tweeting, and posting on Facebook and Instagram. As this information pours in, it is inputted on the map. Volunteer organizations can then access the map to see where help is most needed. "Situational awareness is key to allocating resources and coordinating logistics," says Patrick. "These dynamic, ever-changing maps are like having your own helicopter. They provide a bird's-eye view as events unfold across time and space. Gaining information like this straight from crisis zones is a game changer; these technologies didn't exist just a few years ago."

Who inputs the information as it comes in? The SBTF is a network of people involved in crisis mapping who come from 80 different countries so they can input the information around the clock. More than 800 volunteers are trained, tech-savvy, and ready to work at a moment's notice. They gather the messages, photos, video, and high-resolution satellite images, and integrate them into the Ushahidi map. "These people are passionate about helping and making a difference."

Patrick has figured out how to resolve a problem. By establishing an organizational system that can take incoming information in real time and put it on a map that relief organizations can access, he has figured out a way to get help to the people who need it most.

D. SUMMARIZE Explain to a partner how crisis mapping works.

UNIT 8

Civic Responsibility

A man holds a banner that contains the preamble to the U.S. Constitution.

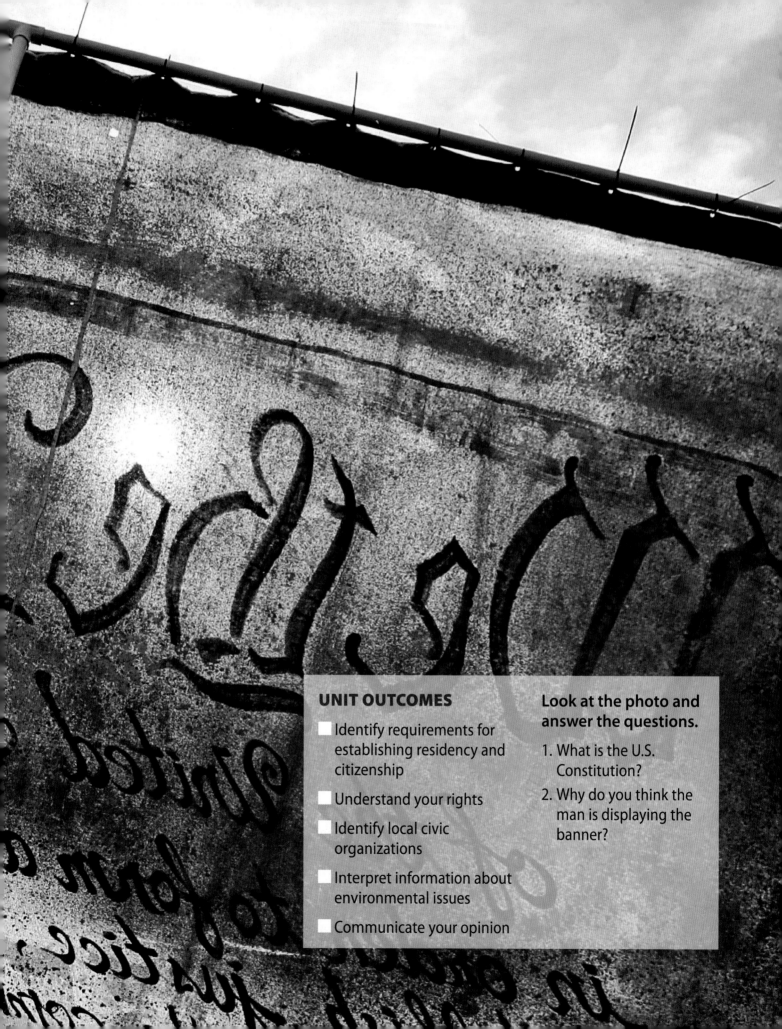

UNIT OUTCOMES

☐ Identify requirements for establishing residency and citizenship

☐ Understand your rights

☐ Identify local civic organizations

☐ Interpret information about environmental issues

☐ Communicate your opinion

Look at the photo and answer the questions.

1. What is the U.S. Constitution?

2. Why do you think the man is displaying the banner?

Vocabulary Builder

A. INFER Guessing the meaning of a word from the context of a sentence is called *making an inference*. Read each sentence and infer the meaning of the italicized word and its part of speech. Then, look each word up in a dictionary.

1. The judge gave an *impartial* verdict that did not favor either side.

   Part of speech: _____ Meaning: _____

   _____

   Dictionary definition: _____

2. There are so many *commuters* on the roads today that there is always a lot of pollution and noise.

   Part of speech: _____ Meaning: _____

   _____

   Dictionary definition: _____

3. We all must *conserve* energy so that we can protect the environment for our kids.

   Part of speech: _____ Meaning: _____

   _____

   Dictionary definition: _____

4. During the war, many *refugees* went to safer countries to live better lives.

   Part of speech: _____ Meaning: _____

   _____

   Dictionary definition: _____

5. She runs a *charitable* organization that gives food to homeless people.

   Part of speech: _____ Meaning: _____

   _____

   Dictionary definition: _____

B. Each sentence in Exercise A reflects the topic of a lesson in this unit. Look at the sentences and guess what you think each lesson will be about.

1. _____

2. _____

3. _____

4. _____

5. _____

C. **CLASSIFY** Look at the list of terms. Categorize each term by writing it under the correct lesson title.

alien	conserve	punishment	reusable
bear arms	eligible	refugee	slavery
believe	naturalization	peaceably assemble	social welfare
capital crime	opinion	resource	status
civic	protect		

Identify requirements for establishing residency and citizenship	Understand your rights	Identify local civic organizations	Interpret information about environmental issues	Communicate your opinion

D. Write your own sentence for each of the words below.

1. naturalization: _____

2. punishment: _____

3. civic: _____

4. reusable: _____

5. resource: _____

LESSON ① Investigating citizenship

GOAL ▨ Identify requirements for establishing residency and citizenship

A. How can an immigrant become a permanent resident of the United States? Make a list of your ideas below.

1. _____
2. _____
3. _____
4. _____

B. **PREDICT** Several students in Mrs. Morgan's class want to become permanent residents of the United States. Read about each nonresident below and decide if you think he or she is eligible to become a permanent resident. Write *yes* or *no*.

1. Hanh has been living in the U.S. since 1995. She recently became engaged to a U.S. citizen. Is she eligible? _____

2. Sadiq is a refugee from Iraq who has been here for six months. Is he eligible? _____

3. Ella is 35 and her mother just became a permanent resident. Is she eligible? _____

4. Phillipe has lived in the U.S. since 1965. Is he eligible?

_____

5. Enrique's wife just became a permanent resident. Is he eligible?

_____

C. Read the following information found on the U.S. Citizenship and Immigration Services website (www.uscis.gov).

You may be *eligible* to apply for adjustment to permanent resident status if you are already in the United States *and* if one or more of the following categories apply to you.

Family Member 1. You are the spouse, parent, unmarried child under age 21, the unmarried son or daughter over age 21, the married son or daughter, or the brother or sister of a United States citizen and have a visa petition approved on your behalf. 2. You are the spouse or unmarried son or daughter of any age of a lawful permanent resident and you have a family-based visa petition approved on your behalf.

Employment You are an alien who has an approved visa petition filed on your behalf by a United States employer.

Fiancé You were a fiancé who was admitted to the United States on a K-1 visa and then married the U.S. citizen *who applied for the K-1 visa for you*. Your unmarried, minor children are also eligible for adjustment of status. If you did not marry the U.S. citizen who filed the K-1 petition on your behalf, or if you married another U.S. citizen or lawful permanent resident, you are not eligible to adjust status in the United States.

Asylee You are an asylee or refugee who has been in the United States for at least a year after being given asylum or refugee status and still qualify for asylum or refugee status.

Diversity Visa You received notice from the Department of State that you have won a visa in the Diversity Visa Lottery.

U.S. Resident Since Before 01/01/72 You have been a continuous resident of the United States since before January 1, 1972.

Parent's Lawful Permanent Resident (LPR) Status Your parent became a lawful permanent resident after you were born. You may be eligible to receive following-to-join benefits if you are the unmarried child under age 21 of the lawful permanent resident. In these cases, you may apply to adjust to permanent resident status at the same time that your parent applies for following-to-join benefits for you.

Spouse's LPR Status Your spouse became a lawful permanent resident after you were married. You may be eligible to receive following-to-join benefits. In these cases, you may apply to adjust to permanent resident status at the same time that your spouse applies for following-to-join benefits for you.

D. **EVALUATE** Look back at each of the nonresidents in Exercise B. Do you need to change some of your answers? Discuss each situation with a partner and decide what specific details would make each person eligible for permanent resident status.

E. Listen to the talk about how to become a citizen. Fill in the missing words.

CD
TR 34

United States (U.S.) citizenship carries many _____ with it. The decision to become a U.S. citizen is a very important one. Being granted U.S. citizenship is known as _____. In most cases, a person who wants to naturalize must first be a _____ resident. By becoming a U.S. citizen, you gain many _____ that permanent residents or others do not have, including the _____. To be eligible for naturalization, you must first meet certain _____ set by U.S. law.

What are the basic requirements to apply for naturalization?

Generally, to be eligible for naturalization you must:

• Be age _____ or older; and

• Be a permanent resident for a certain amount of time (usually five years); and

• Be a person of good _____ character; and

• Have a basic knowledge of U.S. _____ and government; and

• Have a period of _____ residence and physical presence in the U.S.; and

• Be able to read, _____, and speak basic English. There are exceptions to this rule for someone who:

  – Is _____ years old and has been a permanent resident for at least 15 years; or

  – Is _____ years old and has been a permanent resident for at least 20 years; or

  – Has a physical or mental impairment that makes them unable to _____ these requirements.

When can I apply for naturalization?

You may be able to apply for naturalization if you are at least 18 years of age and have been a permanent resident of the U.S.:

• For at least _____ years; or

• For at least _____ years during which time you have been, and continue to be, married to and living in marriage with your U.S. citizen husband or wife; or

• Have honorable service in the U.S. military. Certain _____ of U.S. citizens and members of the military may be able to file for naturalization sooner than noted above previously.

F. **ANALYZE** How many requirements are there to apply for naturalization? What are they? Discuss with a partner.

G. Do you know people who have become permanent residents or citizens? Write short paragraphs about them on a separate piece of paper.

LESSON ② Rights

GOAL ▓ Understand your rights

A. SUMMARIZE In 1791, the Bill of Rights was added to the United States Constitution. Read and paraphrase the first 10 amendments.

Amendment I Congress shall make no law respecting an establishment of religion, or prohibiting the free exercise thereof; or abridging the freedom of speech, or of the press; or the right of the people peaceably to assemble, and to petition the government for a redress of grievances.

Amendment II A well regulated militia, being necessary to the security of a free state, the right of the people to keep and bear arms, shall not be infringed.

Amendment III No soldier shall, in time of peace be quartered in any house, without the consent of the owner, nor in time of war, but in a manner to be prescribed by law.

Amendment IV The right of the people to be secure in their persons, houses, papers, and effects, against unreasonable searches and seizures, shall not be violated, and no warrants shall issue, but upon probable cause, supported by oath or affirmation, and particularly describing the place to be searched, and the persons or things to be seized.

Amendment V No person shall be held to answer for a capital, or otherwise infamous crime, unless on a presentment or indictment of a grand jury, except in cases arising in the land or naval forces, or in the militia, when in actual service in time of war or public danger; nor shall any person be subject for the same offense to be twice put in jeopardy of life or limb; nor shall be compelled in any criminal case to be a witness against himself, nor be deprived of life, liberty, or property, without due process of law; nor shall private property be taken for public use, without just compensation.

Amendment VI In all criminal prosecutions, the accused shall enjoy the right to a speedy and public trial, by an impartial jury of the state and district wherein the crime shall have been committed, which district shall have been previously ascertained by law, and to be informed of the nature and cause of the accusation; to be confronted with the witnesses against him; to have compulsory process for obtaining witnesses in his favor, and to have the assistance of counsel for his defense.

Amendment VII In suits at common law, where the value in controversy shall exceed twenty dollars, the right of trial by jury shall be preserved, and no fact tried by a jury, shall be otherwise reexamined in any court of the United States, than according to the rules of the common law.

Amendment VIII Excessive bail shall not be required, nor excessive fines imposed, nor cruel and unusual punishments inflicted.

Amendment IX The enumeration in the Constitution, of certain rights, shall not be construed to deny or disparage others retained by the people.

Amendment X The powers not delegated to the United States by the Constitution, nor prohibited by it to the states, are reserved to the states respectively, or to the people.

B. Match each amendment with the right it guarantees.

1. The first amendment guarantees _____.

2. The second amendment guarantees _____.

3. The third amendment guarantees _____.

4. The fourth amendment guarantees _____.

5. The fifth amendment guarantees _____.

6. The sixth amendment guarantees _____.

7. The seventh amendment guarantees _____.

8. The eighth amendment guarantees _____.

9. The ninth amendment guarantees _____.

10. The tenth amendment guarantees _____.

a. a speedy and public trial by an impartial jury

b. the right to be charged by a grand jury if accused of a serious crime

c. people have other rights not listed in the Bill of Rights

d. freedom of religion

e. people, homes, and belongings are protected from unreasonable search and seizure

f. right to keep and bear arms

g. people have all the rights not given to the government by the Constitution

h. that government cannot force people to house soldiers during times of peace

i. a trial by jury in civil cases (dispute between private parties or between the government and a private party)

j. no excessive bail or fines will be imposed and that punishment will not be cruel and unusual

C. DETERMINE Read each situation. Then, decide which amendment describes your rights. Write the amendment numbers on the lines.

1. Your friend is Christian and celebrates Easter, but you are Jewish. _____

2. You have a registered gun in your house, locked up in a safe. _____

3. The police can't come into your home without a warrant. _____

4. If you are convicted of a crime, your punishment will not be cruel. _____

5. If you are accused of a crime, you will get a fair trial. _____

D. INTERPRET There is currently a total of 27 amendments to the Constitution. Read about four of the amendments and answer the questions that follow.

Amendment XIII (1865)

Neither slavery nor involuntary servitude, except as a punishment for crime whereof the party shall have been duly convicted, shall exist within the United States, or any place subject to their jurisdiction.

Amendment XV (1870)

The right of citizens of the United States to vote shall not be denied or abridged by the United States or by any state on account of race, color, or previous condition of servitude.

Amendment XIX (1920)

The right of citizens of the United States to vote shall not be denied or abridged by the United States or by any state on account of sex.

Amendment XXVI (1971)

The right of citizens of the United States, who are 18 years of age or older, to vote, shall not be denied or abridged by the United States or any state on account of age.

1. What does the thirteenth amendment guarantee? _____

2. The fifteenth, nineteenth, and twenty-sixth amendments are all about the same right.

   What is it? _____

3. What is the difference between these three amendments?

   _____

   _____

4. In the original Constitution, why do you think so many groups of people were not given the

   right to vote? _____

   _____

E. ANALYZE Discuss the following in a small group.

Do any of the rights identified in this lesson affect your life? Which ones? In what ways?

F. Create a Bill of Rights for your classroom or school.

LESSON **3** Getting involved

GOAL ▓ Identify local civic organizations

A. Read about civic organizations.

A civic organization is a group of people who come together for educational or charitable purposes, including the promotion of community welfare. The money generated by these clubs is devoted exclusively to charitable, educational, recreational, or social welfare purposes.

B. Read about a civic organization.

The Mothers' Club of Northville, Michigan

The Mothers' Club is a group of 35 dynamic women working to help Northville school children excel by providing enrichment materials and opportunities.

History

In 1935, a group of 12 women decided to meet regularly for enlightenment and social activities. During the Depression of the 1930s, the Mothers' Club held a fundraiser to purchase milk for schoolchildren to drink with their lunches. The Club's fundraising has now grown to three events each year, enabling the Club to donate approximately $30,000 annually to student enrichment programs and activities.

Fundraising

A. Fall: The Mothers' Club hosts a booth during Northville's Victorian Festival.

B. Winter: *All Aglow* is an opportunity to honor or remember someone by purchasing a light on the community Christmas tree, located in front of the bandshell in downtown Northville.

C. Spring: *Hands to the Future*, a dinner and auction held annually in March, alternates every other year with *The Community Telephone Directory*, distributed biannually to every household in the Northville School District.

Community Service

The Mothers' Club performs service projects at the public school buildings on a rotating cycle, working at two or three schools each year.

Social

1. Book club
2. Lunch and movie afternoons
3. Evening socials
4. Weekend getaways

C. Answer the following questions with a partner. Share your answers with others in your class.

1. What makes the Mothers' Club a civic organization?

2. What civic organizations are there in your community?

D. Read about the civic organizations and answer the questions on the next page.

 **American Legion**

Purpose: To provide care for veterans and their families at hospitals and homes in the community
Members: Relatives of veterans
Annual Dues: Amounts vary

 **Boy Scouts**

Purpose: To promote self-confidence, service to others, citizenship, and outdoor skills
Members: Boys only, at least 11 years old
Volunteer Scoutmasters: Male and female scoutmasters needed
Annual Dues: $24

 **Friends of the Library**

Purpose: To promote and support the local public library
Members: All welcome
Annual Dues: $15

 **Hiking Club**

Purpose: To enjoy the outdoors and also help raise public awareness of issues that face the present-day outdoors
Members: Anyone who enjoys hiking
Annual Dues: $10

 **Garden Club**

Purpose: To share experiences in gardening
Members: Anyone who enjoys gardening
Annual Dues: $15
Special Events: Plant sale

 **Rotary Club**

Purpose: To provide humanitarian service, encourage high ethical standards in all vocations, and help build goodwill and peace in the world
Members: To become a Rotarian, you must be invited to join a Rotary Club by a member of that club. A qualified candidate for Rotary Club membership is an adult of good character and good business, professional, or community reputation.
Annual Dues: Amounts vary

1. Which clubs would you join if you liked nature? _____

2. Which clubs can you join if you are a woman? _____
   _____

3. Of those which have them, which club has the highest dues? _____

   The lowest? _____

4. Which clubs provide community service? _____
   _____

5. If you could join one club, which one would it be? _____

   Why? _____

E. **Some of the students from Mrs. Morgan's class want to create a civic organization. They have come together because they have common interests. Read about the students below and then come up with ideas for their organization.**

> Hanh, Sadiq, Ella, Phillipe, and Enrique have just found out that many students at their school can't afford to buy books. There are over 100 students a year who attend class without textbooks. Hanh, Sadiq, Ella, Phillipe, and Enrique have one thing in common—they are all very creative. Sadiq takes beautiful photographs, Hanh and Ella both knit; they can make anything from hats to sweaters and blankets, Phillipe is an accomplished musician and songwriter, and Enrique paints oil paintings of flowers and animals.

Name of civic organization: _____

Purpose: _____

Members: _____

Annual dues: _____

Special events: _____

F. **CREATE** **Follow the directions for creating a civic organization.**

Step 1. Get together with a few students from your class and create a new civic organization. Complete the information about your organization below.

- Name of civic organization
- Purpose
- Members
- Annual dues
- Special events

Step 2. Recruit members for your organization. You need at least ten members to be a true organization.

GOAL ▮ Interpret information about environmental issues

A. EVALUATE Look at the list of ways to create less trash. Which ones do you do? Put a check (✓) next to them.

☐ Buy items in bulk from loose bins when possible to reduce the packaging wasted.
☐ Avoid products with several layers of packaging when only one is sufficient.
☐ Buy products that you can reuse.
☐ Maintain and repair durable products instead of buying new ones.
☐ Check reports for products that are easily repaired and have low breakdown rates.
☐ Reuse items like bags and containers when possible.
☐ Use cloth napkins instead of paper ones.
☐ Use reusable plates and utensils instead of disposable ones.
☐ Use reusable containers to store food instead of aluminum foil and cling wrap.
☐ Shop with a canvas bag instead of using paper and plastic bags.
☐ Buy rechargeable batteries for devices used frequently.
☐ Reuse packaging cartons and shipping materials. Old newspapers make great packaging material.
☐ Buy used furniture—there is a surplus of it, and it is much cheaper than new furniture.

B. Interview your partner to find out how he or she conserves energy at home. Put a check (✓) next to the ones he or she does.

☐ Clean or replace air filters on your air-conditioning unit at least once a month.
☐ Lower the thermostat on your water heater to 120°F.
☐ Wrap your water heater in an insulated blanket.
☐ Turn down or shut off your water heater when you will be away for extended periods.
☐ Turn off unneeded lights even when leaving a room for a short time.
☐ Set your refrigerator temperature at 36 to 38°F and your freezer at 0 to 5°F.
☐ When using an oven, minimize door opening while it is in use.
☐ Clean the lint filter in your dryer after every load so that it uses less energy.
☐ Unplug seldom-used appliances.
☐ Use a microwave whenever you can instead of a conventional oven or stove.
☐ Wash clothes with warm or cold water instead of hot.
☐ Turn off lights, computers, and other appliances when not in use.
☐ Use compact fluorescent lightbulbs to save money and energy.
☐ Keep your thermostat at 68°F in winter and 78°F in summer.
☐ Use cold water instead of warm or hot water when possible.
☐ Connect your outdoor lights to a timer.

C. Sustainable Environment for Quality of Life (SEQL) has put together several action items that they would like to see accomplished in their communities in North and South Carolina. Read their plan for carpooling.

Carpooling: What is it?

Vanpooling/carpooling is an arrangement by a group of commuters to ride together from home or a prearranged meeting place in a van or a car to their destinations in a single round trip, with the driver as a fellow commuter. Vanpools/carpools usually consist of individuals who live near each other and are employees of the same company, or are employees of different companies located only a short distance apart, and have the same work hours. The great advantage of vanpools and carpools is that it reduces vehicle trips, reduces vehicle miles traveled, and therefore reduces auto emissions that result in poor air quality.

Shared Impact and Benefits

- Car- and vanpooling reduce overall auto emissions by reducing vehicle miles traveled, and by doing so, improve air quality.
- Peak-hour traffic congestion (and resulting gasoline consumption) are reduced. Nine billion gallons of fuel are wasted in traffic congestion each year.
- Employers will be able to offer employees a value-added benefit and take a tax write-off.
- Eight of ten U.S. workers believe commuter benefits are valuable to employees.
- Furthermore, employers that pay for employee parking costs can save money.
- Vanpool/carpool participants save money by sharing commuting costs.
- Vanpool/carpool riders have less stressful commutes to work. Employers will also have more productive employees with higher morale.

Costs

Usually vanpoolers/carpoolers will share the costs of gasoline, maintenance, and/or leasing the vehicles.

How long does this take to implement?

A vanpooling/carpooling program can be implemented within a few months. Once the program is established, individual pools can be set up in less than a few weeks.

The Bottom Line

Carpooling and vanpooling commuters get to work in ways that reduce air pollution and traffic congestion, save employers and employees money, reduce the environmental impacts associated with driving single-passenger vehicles, reduce parking space demand and expenses, and relieve commuter stress.

Who needs to be involved?

- Governing board and/or management (to endorse a vanpool/carpool policy and support a program that provides incentives for employees who participate in a vanpool or carpool)
- Businesses and their human resource or fiscal office staff
- Transit providers and/or private vanpool leasing companies
- Private parking deck and lot owners
- Employees willing to start up their own vanpool or carpool

D. Working with a partner, choose one of the following three environmental topics. Come up with a list of programs that might work to improve the environment in your community.

air quality

water resources

sustainable development

Topic: _____

Possible programs: _____

_____

_____

_____

E. **DETERMINE** Find another pair of students who chose the same topic as you. Work together and share your ideas. Then, choose one program to develop. Think about and decide on the following items.

Topic: _____

Name of program: _____

Brief description of how the program works: _____

_____

_____

_____

Impact on and benefit to the environment: _____

_____

_____

Length of time to implement: _____

Cost: _____

People involved: _____

LESSON ⑤ Expressing yourself

A. BRAINSTORM Everyone has an opinion when it comes to the environment. In a small group, brainstorm some *yes* and *no* opinions for each of the suggestions below.

EXAMPLE: People should not be permitted to buy large cars that create a lot of pollution.

Yes: *If everyone bought smaller cars, pollution would be significantly reduced.*

No: *Many people need large cars for their families. Large cars are safer and hold more people and more groceries.*

1. Our city should build more carpool lanes.

Yes	No
a. _____	a. _____
b. _____	b. _____
c. _____	c. _____

2. Everyone should take their own recyclable items to a recycling center.

Yes	No
a. _____	a. _____
b. _____	b. _____
c. _____	c. _____

3. Each home should only be allowed to have a certain amount of water each month.

Yes	No
a. _____	a. _____
b. _____	b. _____
c. _____	c. _____

B. Practice communicating your opinion to a partner. Use the phrases below.

I think . . .	I believe . . .	In my opinion, . . .	I agree.	I disagree.

EXAMPLE: **Student A:** *I think our city should build more carpool lanes.*

Student B: *I disagree. In my opinion, it is a waste of money because it won't make more people carpool.*

C. Ella wrote a paragraph communicating her opinion on the environment. Read.

Our Most Precious Resource

There are many things we should do to protect our environment, but I think one of the most important things we can do is to conserve water. Why? Water is our most precious resource. I believe this for many reasons. One reason is that the human body is made up of 75% water. We can only live for one week without water; therefore, we need to drink water to survive. Another reason that water is so important is that we need it to clean. We need water to clean our bodies, wash our dishes, flush our toilets, and launder our clothes. Can you imagine not being able to do any of these things? Still another reason is that plants and trees need water to grow and survive. Without plants and trees, humans wouldn't survive because plants give off the oxygen we need in order to breathe. For these reasons, I believe that we need to conserve our most precious resource—water.

D. Answer the questions about the sentence types in Ella's paragraph.

1. What is Ella's topic sentence?

   _____

2. What is Ella's concluding sentence?

   _____

3. Ella gives three reasons to support her main idea. For each idea, she gives a supporting detail. What are her reasons and details?

   a. Reason: _____

      Detail: _____

   b. Reason: _____

      Detail: _____

   c. Reason: _____

      Detail: _____

E. ANALYZE Study these transitional expressions with your teacher. Which ones did Ella use in her paragraph?

Transitional Expressions		
One reason	The *first* reason	*Some* people
⇓	⇓	⇓
Another reason	The *second* reason	*Other* people
⇓	⇓	⇓
Still another reason	The *third* reason	*Still* others

- Use these phrases to connect your ideas.
- Choose the set of phrases that works best for your topic.
- Don't shift back and forth among sets of phrases.

F. Choose an environmental issue you feel strongly about. Brainstorm ways to resolve the issue by creating a cluster diagram on a separate piece of paper.

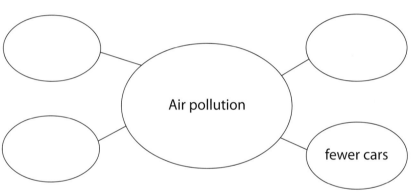

G. Look at your cluster diagram. Write complete sentences for the ways in which your chosen environmental issue can be resolved.

Reason 1: _____

_____

Reason 2: _____

_____

Reason 3: _____

_____

H. COMPOSE On a separate piece of paper, write a paragraph communicating your opinion about the environmental issue you chose in Exercise F.

 # Mom, I'm so proud of you

Before You Watch

A. **Look at the picture and answer the questions.**

1. Where are Hector, Mateo, Naomi, and Mr. and Mrs. Sanchez?

2. Why are there drinks on the table?

While You Watch

B. **Watch the video and complete the dialog.**

Naomi: You mean you've kept your Turkish (1) _citizenship_ this whole time?

Mrs. Sanchez: Yes. I've been a legal permanent (2) _____ until now. Victor was a U.S. citizen, and so is my son. I was busy with my family and my job. The years passed, and I just never took the time to change my status.

Naomi: What made you (3) _____ your mind?

Mrs. Sanchez: Well, now I have more time, and I've been thinking it's more important to

get (4) _____.

Mr. Sanchez: The next presidential (5) _____ is coming up in a couple of years, as you know, and I convinced Miriam that it's important to vote.

Check Your Understanding

C. **What are the steps in the immigration process? Write numbers to show the order.**

a. _____ Take an oath at the immigration ceremony.

b. _____ Wait while officials review your application.

c. __1__ File an immigration application.

d. _____ Meet with an immigration official.

e. _____ When the application is approved, schedule a citizenship test.

f. _____ Take the citizenship test.

Review

Learner Log

I can identify requirements for establishing residency and citizenship.   I can understand my rights.
☐ Yes ☐ No ☐ Maybe   ☐ Yes ☐ No ☐ Maybe

A. **List four ways a person can become a permanent resident of the United States.**

1. _____

2. _____

3. _____

4. _____

B. **List four requirements for becoming a U.S. citizen.**

1. _____

2. _____

3. _____

4. _____

C. **Write the correct amendment number in front of each description.**

1. The _____ amendment is about the abolishment of slavery.

2. The _____ amendment is about the right for women to vote.

3. The _____ amendment is about the right to be charged by a grand jury if accused of a serious crime.

4. The _____ amendment is about protection from unreasonable search and seizure.

5. The _____ amendment is about a trial by jury in civil cases (dispute between private parties or between the government and a private party).

6. The _____ amendment is about a speedy and public trial by an impartial jury.

7. The _____ amendment is about freedom of religion.

8. The _____ amendment is about the right to keep and bear arms.

9. The _____ amendment is about the right for people of all races to vote.

10. The _____ amendment is about protection from forced housing of soldiers.

Learner Log

I can identify local civic organizations.
■ Yes   ■ No   ■ Maybe

I can interpret information about environmental issues.
■ Yes   ■ No   ■ Maybe

I can communicate my opinion.
■ Yes   ■ No   ■ Maybe

D. Create a civic organization for the following group's problem.

> *A group of children who live in a shelter for homeless families goes to a nearby elementary school. However, the parents of the children don't have any money to buy the required school uniform—blue pants and a white shirt. The volunteers at the shelter want to find a way to raise money for these kids.*

Name of organization: _____

Purpose: _____

Members: _____

Annual dues: _____

Special events: _____

E. Work with a partner and list five ways you can help protect and preserve the environment.

1. _____

2. _____

3. _____

4. _____

5. _____

F. Choose one of the ways you can help protect and preserve the environment in Exercise E and write a paragraph about why it is important.

_____

_____

_____

_____

_____

_____

_____

_____

Vocabulary Review

A. Choose five words from the vocabulary list. Use each word in a meaningful sentence that reviews an important point or piece of information that you have learned in this unit.

alien	conserve	protect	reusable
bear arms	eligible	punishment	slavery
believe	naturalization	refugee	social welfare
capital crime	opinion	resource	status
civic	peaceably assemble		

1. _____

2. _____

3. _____

4. _____

5. _____

B. Use five different words from the list above to write five different opinions you have.

1. _____

2. _____

3. _____

4. _____

5. _____

C. Write the correct word in front of each definition below.

1. _____ means resident foreigner.

2. _____ means having the right to do or be chosen for something.

3. _____ means a payment for doing something wrong.

4. _____ means useful things.

5. _____ means a legal condition.

In this project, you will work individually to develop an opinion speech supported with details.

1. Look back at everything you have learned in this unit and choose one topic to give a speech about. Remember, this speech should be persuasive. You should not just present facts without giving your opinion. However, you can support your opinion with facts. First, write one sentence that states your opinion.

   Some examples:

   - *I think that someone should be able to become a citizen anytime he or she wants.*

   - *I don't think Americans should have the right to bear arms.*

   - *I think every citizen should have to be a part of a civic organization.*

2. Read your opinion out loud to the class.

3. Come up with reasons to support your opinion and write a speech. Prepare to speak for at least two minutes.

4. Practice your speech. Remember the following tips:

   - Enunciate (speak clearly).

   - Make eye contact with your audience.

   - Practice so you recall your major points without notes.

   - Thank your audience for listening and/or for their time.

5. Give your two-minute opinion speech. At the end of your speech, ask your classmates if they have any questions.

A woman takes a selfie after becoming a citizen of the United States.

Women at the Forefront

" In countries where women have so many rights and advantages, many are looking for a sense of purpose. Can you imagine if you took even a little bit of that energy and put it into something that helps another person?"
—Roshini Thinakaran

A. PREDICT What do these women have in common?

1. A widow worked as a housekeeper to provide for her family. She then went back to school to get a higher-paying job.

2. A woman was forced to leave school and work as a carpet weaver. She is now working as an editor for a women's magazine and finishing school.

3. Women are fighting to escape being servants.

4. A woman helped start a center that provides medical, psychological, and legal aid to victims of torture and violence.

B. Read about Roshini Thinakaran.

Roshini Thinakaran was born in Sri Lanka, but she was raised in the United States. She studied at George Mason University in Virginia, where she received a bachelor's in communication and minored in journalism. As a filmmaker, Roshini's work currently involves profiling women in war-torn countries. I had a chance to sit down with her and to talk about the impact she is making on the lives of others.

Interviewer: Roshini, your work takes you to different countries affected by war. Where have you traveled to do your research?

Roshini: My research has taken me to Sri Lanka, Iraq, Liberia, Afghanistan, and Sudan.

Interviewer: Tell us about the women you have met.

Roshini: Often without electricity or water, women go on with their lives. They get groceries, cook dinner, and take their kids to school. But an element of danger is always with them. They're always in survival mode.

Interviewer: Are these women unique?

Roshini: No. Aspirations are universal. They all want their kids to get an education, have enough to eat, be safe, and enjoy a happy life. Just because they were born in a war zone or refugee camp, they still fall in love, care about their families, and have dreams.

Interviewer: So you are using these women's stories in your film project?

Roshini: Yes. My film project is called Women at the Forefront. This film project is now turning into a television series. I've focused on a particular theme for each country, but the overall picture I reveal is a strong women's movement—born of oppression and hardship—happening all around the world. Unlike movements where women were striving for equal rights, these women strive for basic rights.

Interviewer: What is your goal?

Roshini: My goal is to bring awareness of women who are making real strides and to eventually build schools in these countries, for both girls and boys. If you don't empower people with education, societies will break down.

Interviewer: Do you hope to achieve something more than just awareness with this project?

Roshini: I want this project to connect women who have more economic and educational opportunities with women who are struggling to reshape war-torn nations. In countries where women have so many rights and advantages, many are looking for a sense of purpose. Can you imagine if you took even a little bit of that energy and put it into something that helps another person?

C. CREATE The women you read about in Exercise A are women that Roshini highlights in her film series. Choose one of the women and write her story as you imagine it. Be creative!

One Village Makes a Difference

Sometimes the Yamuna River looks like a science project.

In the last four units, you have learned about health and environmental issues. You have also explored the ways you can help. For people who live along the Yamuna River in northern India, their health is at risk from unclean water. You will now learn about what some individuals are doing to help change that.

Before You Watch

A. Read the sentences. Then, match each word with the correct meaning.

1. The Yamuna is the longest river in northern India.
2. Even though it is very hot, many people live in the Thar Desert.
3. The visibility in New Delhi is very poor because the smog is so bad.
4. The villagers built a dam to bring more water to the fields.
5. The villagers get their drinking water from a well.

_____ desert   a. huge cloud of dirty air

_____ river   b. area of very hot, dry land

_____ dam   c. barrier to stop a river from moving

_____ pit   d. deep hole in the ground to hold water

_____ smog   e. large amount of moving water

B. Circle the caption that best describes each picture. Then, compare your answers with a partner.

1. New Delhi has many restaurants and shopping centers.
2. Sometimes there isn't enough water for everyone.
3. Heavy smog fills the sky above the city.

1. Industrial waste is thrown into the river every day.
2. Wells help villagers water their farms.
3. Temperatures frequently reach 100° F.

1. Villagers walk for miles to get water.
2. Water trucks deliver water to surrounding towns.
3. New Delhi is a large city in northern India.

While You Watch

WORD FOCUS

Industrial waste is the unwanted material that factories produce when manufacturing something. This can be oil, chemicals, plastic, glass, paper, metal, etc.

A. Watch the video and circle the items you see.

hospital	river	farms	dam
water truck	animals	classroom	desert
car accident	cooking	shopping center	people playing soccer

B. Read the sentences. Circle *T* if sentences are true or *F* if they are false. Correct the false sentences in your notebook.

1. The people of New Delhi need around eight billion gallons of water each day.   T   F

2. Even expensive restaurants in New Delhi depend on trucks to bring them water.   T   F

3. Villagers often have to share their drinking water with animals.   T   F

4. Some people believe that India's large dams have dried up the rivers.   T   F

5. Rajendra Singh encourages villagers to use modern technology to find water.   T   F

C. Watch the video again. Choose the correct word to complete each sentence.

environmentalist	one billion	14 million
monsoon	science experiment	

1. New Delhi residents need _____ gallons of water each day.

2. The Yamuna River sometimes looks like a _____.

3. About _____ people live in and around New Delhi.

4. A heavy rain that comes once a year is called a _____.

5. Rajendra Singh is a(n) _____.

After You Watch

A. How do the villagers make small earthen dams? Put the steps in the correct order.

_____ Wait for rain to raise the water levels.

_____ Dig a small hole or pit.

_____ Save the water in wells or reservoirs.

_____ Water the plants in the fields.

_____ Make a layer of rocks and stones.

_____ Collect rocks and stones.

B. How do you use water? Complete the table with your own information. Then, share your answers in small groups.

Activity	Sunday	Monday	Tuesday	Wednesday	Thursday	Friday	Saturday
Taking a shower	✓	✓	✓	✓	✓	✓	✓

C. Discuss the questions with a partner and share your answers with the class.

EXAMPLE   Do you ever use more water than you should?
I take very long showers in the morning. I probably use a lot of water.

1. Where does your drinking water come from?
2. What would you do if you had no running water?
3. How could you reduce the amount of water that you use?
4. When do you see people wasting water in your community? Can you think of any examples?

STAND OUT VOCABULARY LIST

PRE-UNIT
cook, 7
do crossword puzzles, 7
do yoga, 7
draw, 7
knit, 7
lift weights, 7
paint, 7
play soccer, 7
play video games, 7
read, 7
run, 7
swim, 7
take pictures, 7
watch movies, 7
write, 7

UNIT 1
achieve, 15, 34
auditory, 15
balance, 15, 34
be flexible, 15, 34
bodily, 15, 19
career path, 14, 15
computer programmer, 14
earning power, 15, 34
educational
    attainment, 15, 34
evaluate, 15, 34
financial, 14
fun, 14
goal setting, 15
graphic designer, 14
inspire, 15, 34
intelligences, 15
interpersonal, 15, 19
intrapersonal, 15, 19
joy, 14
kinesthetic, 15, 19
learning style, 14, 15
linguistic, 15, 19
logical, 15, 19
long-term, 15, 34
mathematical, 19
monitor, 15, 34
motivate, 15, 34
motivation, 14, 15
multiple, 15
musical, 19
naturalistic, 15, 19
photographer, 14

positive outlook, 15, 34
prioritize, 15, 34
pursue, 15, 34
registered nurse, 14
rhythmic, 15, 19
short-term, 15, 34
spatial, 15, 19
support, 15, 34
tactile, 14, 15
time with family, 14
verbal, 15, 19
visual, 14, 15, 19

UNIT 2
bankruptcy, 41
bargain, 60
budget cut, 40
buy in bulk, 40
capital gains, 40, 48
collateral, 41
commit fraud, 40
convert, 48, 60
counterfeit, 60
counterfeit checks, 40
current income, 40
daunting, 41
debt, 60
delinquent, 60
delinquent accounts, 40
dumpster diving, 54
earnings, 60
expense, 60
false pretenses, 40
fraud, 60
inflation, 41, 48
investment, 41
liquid, 41, 48
net appreciation, 48
penalty, 41, 48
periodically, 41
phishing, 54
pretexting, 54
purchasing power, 48
risk, 60
risky, 41, 48
skimming, 54
unauthorized
    transactions, 40
value, 48
vehicle, 48
worth, 60

UNIT 3
accident, 67
air filter, 71
alternator, 71
battery, 71
bodily injury, 67
brake fluid reservoir, 71
change, 67, 84
check, 84
children, 80
choose, 67
collision, 67, 86
commute, 67
convertible, 66
coolant reservoir, 71
coverage, 67
disc brake, 71
distributor, 71
do, 67
exhaust manifold, 71
fatalities, 86
fill, 84
fill up, 67
find, 67
four-door sedan, 66
fuel injection system, 71
imagine, 67
incident, 67
inspect, 84
limits of liability, 67
look at, 67
make, 67
minivan, 66
model, 67
MPG, 86
muffler, 71
odometer, 86
pedestrians, 80
perform, 84
pickup truck, 66
police officer, 80
policy, 67
power steering reservoir, 71
premium, 67, 86
radiator, 71
rear axle, 71
rear suspension, 71
red light, 80
replace, 67, 84
school bus, 80
seat belts, 80

speed limit, 80
sports car, 66
sport utility vehicle
    (SUV), 66
station wagon, 66
stop sign, 80
timing belt, 71
top off, 84
two-door coupe, 66
uninsured motorist, 67
unrestrained, 86
van, 66
VIN, 67
water pump, 71

UNIT 4
abandon, 92
activate, 93
burglarize, 92
burglary, 112
compensate, 93
crime, 92
deteriorate, 93
disturbance, 92
dwelling, 92, 112
enticing, 92
estimate, 93
evident, 92
exterior, 92
get, 95
grounds, 92
have, 95
help, 95
let, 95
litigate, 93
make, 95
policy, 112
possess, 93
premises, 92
premium, 112
prevent, 112
responsibility, 112
responsible, 92
right, 112
seize, 92
summon, 92
terminate, 93
theft, 92
thief, 92
vacate, 93, 112
weapons, 92

STAND OUT GRAMMAR REFERENCE

Review: *Be*

Subject	*Past*	Present	Future
I	was	am	will be
You	were	are	will be
He, She, It	was	is	will be
We	were	are	will be
They	were	are	will be

Review: Simple Tenses

Subject	Past	Present	Future	
I	spent	spend	will spend	more time with my brothers.
You	enjoyed	enjoy	will enjoy	being a mother.
He, She, It	studied	studies	will study	English every day.
We	put	put	will put	our studies first.
They	worked	work	will work	too many hours.

Future Perfect Tense

Subject	*will have*	Past participle		Future event—Time expression
I	will have	become	a teacher	by the time my kids are in school.
He	will have	been	a graphic designer (for five years)	when he turns 35.
They	will have	found	a job	by 2015.

We use the future perfect to talk about an activity that will be completed before another time or event in the future. |—present   ✕—future to be completed (perfect)   ✕—future event with time expression

Note: The order of events is not important. If the future event with the time expression comes first, use a comma.

Example: *By the time my kids are in school, I will have become a teacher.*

Past Perfect Continuous Tense

	First event in past				Second event in past
Subject	*had*	*been*	**Verb + -ing**		
Kimla	had	been	buying	designer clothes	before she started bargain shopping.
He	had	been	buying	coffee at a coffee shop	before he began making it at home.
They	had	been	paying	a lower deductible	before they called the insurance company.

- We use the past perfect continuous to talk about an activity that was happening for a while before another event happened in the past. For the most recent event, we use the simple past tense.
- Remember to use a comma if you put the second event as the first part of the sentence. Example: Before she started bargain shopping, Kimla had been buying designer clothes.

Causative Verbs: *Get, Have, Help, Make, Let*

Subject	**Verb**	**Noun/Pronoun**	**Infinitive (Omit *to* except with *get*.)**
He	will get	his handyman	to come.
She	had	her mom	wait for the repairperson.
The landlord	helped	me	move in.
Ming Mei	makes	her sister	pay half of the rent.
Mr. Martin	let	Ming Mei	skip one month's rent.

Adverb Clauses of Concession

Dependent clause	Independent clause
Although he spends a lot of time in Las Vegas,	he says he doesn't have a gambling problem.
Even though her sister spends thousands of dollars a month,	she doesn't think she is a shopaholic.
Though she has to drink two cups of coffee before she can get out of bed in the morning,	she is convinced she isn't addicted to caffeine.
In spite of the fact that he plays video games for three hours a night,	he denies he has a problem.

Explanation: Adverb clauses of concession show a contrast in ideas. The main or independent clauses show the unexpected outcome. The unexpected outcome in the third example is that it is surprising that she thinks she isn't addicted to caffeine.

Note: The clauses can be reversed and have the same meaning. Do not use a comma if the independent clause comes first in the sentence.

Example: *She doesn't think she is a shopaholic even though she spends thousands of dollars a month.*

Appositives

Noun or Noun Phrase	Appositive	Remainder of sentence (Predicate)
The ad,	**the one with all the great pictures,**	makes me want to buy those dishes.
That computer,	**the fastest machine in the store,**	sells for over $2,000.

Explanation:
- An appositive is a noun or noun phrase that renames another noun next to it in a sentence.
- The appositive adds extra descriptive detail, explains, or identifies something about the noun.

Example: *A helpful gift, money is always appreciated by a newly married couple.*
- An appositive can come before or after the noun phrase it is modifying:

Note: Appositives are usually set off by commas.

Noun Clauses as Objects

Subject + Verb	Noun clause	Explanation
I did	*what* I was asked.	
She knows	*how* the computer works.	• A noun clause starts with a question word or *that* and is followed by a subject and verb.
They decided	*where* the location would be.	
My boss asked	*who* would be best for the job.	• In these examples, the noun clauses are the objects of the sentences.
I hope	*that* they work as a team.	

Transitional Expressions

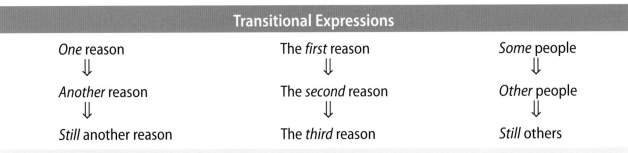

- Use these phrases to connect your ideas.
- Choose the set of phrases that works best for your topic.
- Don't shift back and forth among sets of phrases.

TEXT CREDITS

20 "Educational Attainment and Earning Power for Men and Women 18 and Over" chart. **Source:** Current Population Survey, U.S. Department of Labor, U.S. Bureau of Labor Statistics **Website:** http://www.bls.gov/emp/ep_table_001.htm; **51** "The Four Keys to Great Credit" **Source:** MSN Money **Website:** money.msn.com; **81** "Seat Belt Use in the States, U.S. Territories, and Nationwide, 2006–2013" **Source:** Seat Belt Use in 2013—Use Rates in the States and Territories, National Highway Traffic Safety Administration **Website:** http://www-nrd.nhtsa.dot.gov/Pubs/812030.pdf; **82** "Facts on alcohol-related accidents" Source: Centers for Disease Control and Prevention **Website:** http://www.cdc.gov/motorvehiclesafety/index.html; **107** "Theft prevention newsletter" Source: Burglary Prevention, Jefferson County Sherriff's Department, MO **Website:** http://www.jcsd.org/burglary_prevention.htm; **130** "Percentage of persons without health insurance, by age group using three measures of non-coverage, and percentage of persons with health insurance at the time of interview, by coverage type and age group: United States, January–March 2014" **Source:** Health Insurance Coverage: Early Release of Estimates From the National Health Interview Survey, January–March 2014 **Website:** http://www.cdc.gov/nchs/data/nhis/earlyrelease/insur201409.pdf; **131** "Percentage of persons under age 65 without health insurance coverage at the time of interview, by age group and sex: United States, January–March 2014" **Source:** Health Insurance Coverage: Early Release of Estimates From the National Health Interview Survey, January–March 2014 **Website:** http://www.cdc.gov/nchs/data/nhis/earlyrelease/insur201409.pdf; **132** "Percentage of persons aged 18–64 who lacked health insurance coverage, had public health coverage, and had private health insurance coverage at the time of interview, by selected demographic characteristics: United States, January—March 2014" **Source:** Health Insurance Coverage: Early Release of Estimates From the National Health Interview Survey, January–March 2014 **Website:** http://www.cdc.gov/nchs/data/nhis/earlyrelease/insur201409.pdf; **141** "Health Insurance Coverage of Low Income Adults 19–64" (2013) **Source:** Kaiser Family Foundation estimates based on the Census Bureau's March 2014 Current Population Survey (CPS: Annual Social and Economic Supplements). **Website:** http://kff.org/other/state-indicator/low-income-adults/?state=NY; **185** "Conflict Resolution: Resolving Conflict Rationally and Effectively" **Source:** Mind Tools **Website:** http://mindtools.com; **203–204** "U.S. Citizenship and Immigration Services" **Source:** USCIS **Website:** http://uscis.com; **208** "The Mothers' Club of Northville" **Source:** City of Northville, MI **Website:** http://ci.northville.mi.us; **211** "Create Less Trash" **Source:** Sustainable Environment for Quality of Life **Website:** http://www.centralina.org/; **212** "Carpooling—What is it?" **Source:** Sustainable Environment for Quality of Life **Website:** http://www.centralina.org/

PHOTO CREDITS

Cover: Seth Joel/Getty Images, **Bottom Images** (Left to Right) Jay B Sauceda/Getty Images; Tripod/Getty Images; Portra Images/Getty Images; Portra Images/Getty Images; Mark Edward Atkinson/Tracey Lee/Getty Images; Hero Images/Getty Images; Jade/Getty Images; James Porter/Getty Images; LWA/Larry Williams/Getty Images; Dimitri Otis/Getty Images, **2** (tl) (tc) Portra Images/Getty Images, (tr) Mark Edward Atkinson/Tracey Lee/Getty Images, (cl) Hero Images/Getty Images, (c) Jade/Getty Images, (cr) Seth Joel/Getty Images, **6** (tl) SINITAR/Shutterstock.com, (tc) Comet/Corbis, (tr) Yasser Chalid/Moment Open/Getty Images, **11** kupicoo/iStock/Getty Images, **12–13** Jianan Yu/Reuters, **14** (tl) StockLite/Shutterstock.com, (tr) Juanmonino/E+/Getty Images, (bl) en Pipe Photography/Cultura RM/Getty Images, (br) michaeljung/Shutterstock.com, **18** Yang Liu/Corbis, **25** phipatbig/Shutterstock.com, **28** (tl) StockLite/Shutterstock.com, (tr) Nadino/Shutterstock.com, (cl) Photography/Cultura RM/Getty Images, (cr) Juanmonino/E+/Getty Images, (br) michaeljung/Shutterstock.com, (bl) Fotoluminate LLC/Shutterstock.com, **31** © Cengage Learning, **36** Marco Grob/National Geographic Creative, **38–39** © Kyle Damon Parr, **40** David Molina G/Shutterstock.com, **45** Lightspring/Shutterstock.com, **54** (tl) jason cox/Shutterstock.com, (tc) Jose Luis Pelaez Inc/Getty Images, (tr) maxuser/Shutterstock.com, (b) Image Source/Corbis, **57** © Cengage Learning, **62** Matthew Muspratt/National Geographic Creative, **64–65** Alexander Koerner/Getty Images, **66** kokandr/Shutterstock.com, **68** kokandr/Shutterstock.com, **71** Rawpixel.com/Shutterstock.com, **73** Comet/Corbis, **80** (tl to br) Federal Highway Administration-MUTCD/

Wikimedia Commons; Manual on Uniform Traffic Control Devices for Streets and Highways-2003 Edition/Wikimedia Commons; Wikimedia Commons; MUTCD/Wikimedia Commons; Yield_sign.svg/Wikimedia Commons; Wikimedia Commons; Government of Ontario/Wikimedia Commons; Federal Highway Administration-MUTCD/http://mutcd.fhwa.dot.gov/pdfs/2009r1r2/part2c.pdf/Wikimedia Commons; Road-sign-no-entry.svg: Peeperman/derivative work/Wikipedia Commons; MUTCD/Wikimedia Commons, Fry1989/Wikipedia Commons, **83** © Cengage Learning, **86** Rawpixel.com/Shutterstock.com, **88** Jin-Song Hu/National Geographic Creative, **90–91** Peter Stewart/500px, **94** Forestpath/Dreamstime.com, **102** (tl) Valery Sidelnykov/Shutterstock.com, (tc) Banner/Shutterstock.com, (tr) Stefan90/Getty Images, (cl) ilbusca/Getty Images, (c) Stephen Dalton/ Minden Pictures/Getty Images, (cr) Blend/Corbis, **106** Jon Bilous/Shutterstock.com, **107** sdecoret/Shutterstock.com, **108** SweetBabeeJay/Thinkstock, **109** © Cengage Learning, **114** (t) NASA/Adams Constance/National Geographic Creative, (br) Education Images/Universal Images Group/Getty Images, **116** Tim Laman/National Geographic Creative, **120–121** © Petravb, **124** (cl) Noel Hendrickson/Getty Images, (c) lightpoet/Shutterstock.com, (cr) MSRPhoto/ iStock/Getty Images Plus/Getty Images, **125** Yeko Photo Studio/Shutterstock.com, **134** Dragon Images/Shutterstock.com, **136** elenabsl/Shutterstock.com, **139** © Cengage Learning, **144** Rebecca Hale/National Geographic Creative, **146–147** Brent Humphreys/Redux, **149** Monkey Business Images/Shutterstock.com, **151** Everything/Shutterstock.

com, **154** Seth Joel/Getty Images, **155** LDprod/Shutterstock.com, **159** Felix Mizioznikov/Shutterstock.com, **162** (cl) Encyclopedia/Corbis, (bl) Encyclopedia/Corbis, **164** XiXinXing/Shutterstock.com, **165** © Cengage Learning, **170** (t) AP Images/Richard Shotwell/Invision, (br) Beverly Joubert/National Geographic Creative, **172–173** Clive Wilkinson, **174** (tl) Africa Studio/Shutterstock.com, (tc) IOvE IOvE/Shutterstock.com, (tr) Spiderstock/Getty Images, (cl) Sylvie Bouchard/Shutterstock.com, (c) andres balcazar/Getty Images, (cr) Merydolla/Shutterstock.com, (bl) MSPhotographic/Shutterstock.com, (bc) Goygel-Sokol Dmitry/Shutterstock.com, **176–177** ©Cengage Learning, **178** FabrikaSimf/Shutterstock.com, **186** Konstantin Chagin/Shutterstock.com, **191** © Cengage Learning, **196** © Kris Krug, **198–199** Luis Sinco/Los Angeles Times/Getty Images, **202** (tl) DragonImages/Getty Images, (cl1) Jetta Productions/Blend Images/Getty Images, (cl2) StockLite/Shutterstock.com, (cl3)Monkey Business Images/Shutterstock.com, (bl) Daniel Ernst/Getty Images, **209** (tl) Bob Kreisel/Alamy Stock Photo, (tr) Terra/Corbis, (cl) seyomedo/Shutterstock.com, (cr) Mojca Odar/Shutterstock.com, (bl) MGP/DigitalVision/Getty Images, (br) Esa Hiltula/Alamy Stock Photo, **213** (tl) Vadim Petrakov/Shutterstock.com, (tc) chaoss/Shutterstock.com, (tr) AVN Photo Lab/Shutterstock.com, **217** © Cengage Learning, **221** Mike Segar/Reuters, **222** Mark Thiessen/National Geographic Creative, **224** Hindustan Times/Getty Images, **225** (t) (c) (b) © National Geographic, **237** Rainer Lesniewski/Shutterstock.com.

STAND OUT SKILLS INDEX

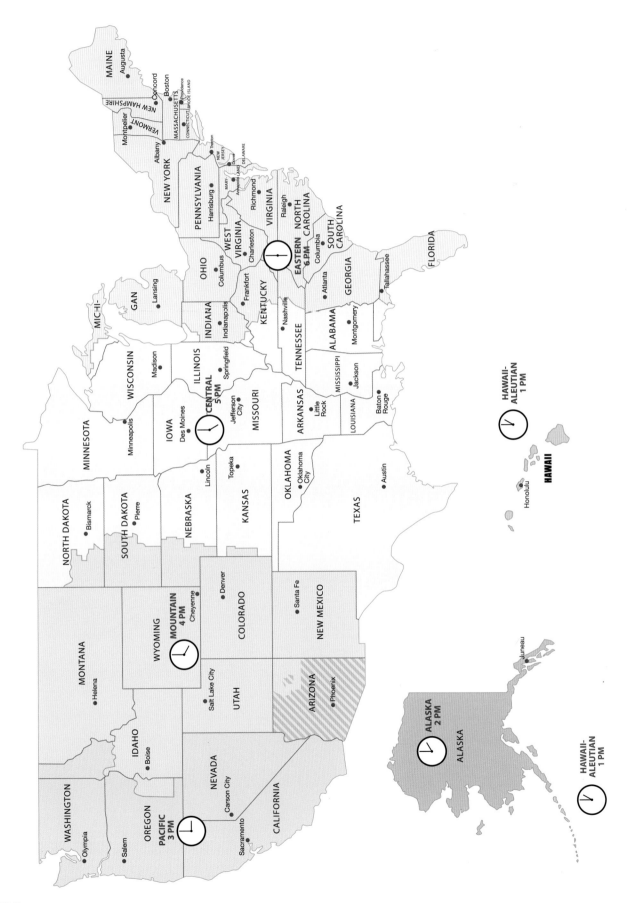